William Morris
on Architecture

William
MORRIS

on Architecture

edited by Chris Miele

Sheffield
Academic Press

Copyright © 1996 Sheffield Academic Press

Published by Sheffield Academic Press Ltd
Mansion House
19 Kingfield Road
Sheffield S11 9AS
England

Printed on acid-free paper in Great Britain
by The Cromwell Press
Melksham, Wiltshire

British Library Cataloguing in Publication Data

A catalogue record for this book is available
from the British Library

ISBN 1-85075-612-0

CONTENTS

INTRODUCTION

Morris's architectural thought does not survive in one piece. It has to be reconstructed from a dozen or so public addresses delivered over the space of about as many years, and then reprinted at various times as pamphlets or in collections, most of which are now hard to find. This collection of his architectural writing makes it possible for readers to judge Morris's contribution to architectural culture for themselves. To present Morris directly, rather than through the medium of his countless interpreters, would seem on the face of it to be an unalloyed good, but there is real risk that this volume will misrepresent him by passing for the book on architecture he never quite got around to writing and in this way invite comparisons. So in fairness it must be said that Morris never defined an architectural theory as neatly or comprehensively as the masters of the *genre* did. This is not to say that his essays are less interesting than those of Pugin, Ruskin, Lethaby, or even, for that matter, Le Corbusier, Venturi, or Rossi, only that the circumstances under which Morris wrote puts his work in a slightly different category. Each piece, being conceived for a separate occasion and, more often than not, for a general audience, had to be developed from first principles. To make his case Morris wrote in a style which was easily accessible. All this gives his writing a freshness and simplicity rare among theoretical heavyweights. Of course much the same could be said of his writings on politics or history, but I fear that in the case of architecture the problem may be more acute, since Morris has been central to our understanding of the development of Modernism in the applied arts. Did what Morris say lead, inevitably, to Walter Gropius, the Bauhaus, and other twentieth-century notions of functional form as Nikolaus Pevsner argued so persuasively some sixty years ago?[1] I would prefer not to try a definitive answer, but my inclination is to say no.

Morris's overriding contribution to nineteenth-century architectural writing was his passion for buildings. In the socialist utopia of the future and the equally ideal world of the medieval past Morris believed that architecture would be and had been a source of intense pleasure, not merely to the people who used it, but more importantly to the people who made it. The pleasure Morris found in medieval architecture was not some anodyne, 'whistle-while-you-work' cheerfulness. It was deep, primitive, erotic, almost beyond the power of language to express. Its character was as intense as real physical love, and if one were minded to write uncharitably about him it might even be linked to fetishism.

Morris would, I am sure, be uncomfortable with this reading since apart from anything else he did not think of himself as an original architectural thinker. Time and time again he told audiences that what he was about to say had been said better before by one writer, John Ruskin, whose chapter from the second volume of the *Stones of Venice* (1853), 'The Nature of Gothic', Morris singled out for praise more than any other work.[2] He liked it so much that he chose it for one of the Kelmscott Press's first publications. In the preface to the 1892 printing Morris described it as 'one of the most important things written by the author ... [and] one of the very few necessary and inevitable utterances of the century'. Now, according to Morris, Ruskin taught him 'that art is the expression of man's pleasure in labour', but, as Mark Swenarton has deftly argued, this line is a creative misreading of Ruskin.[3] The sensuality in Morris is far from well developed in Ruskin who believed only that the workman needed to be happy in order to produce fine work, and in any case when Ruskin talked about pleasure he meant the pleasure to come from looking on works of art not from making them. Morris's architectural philosophy, if we can call it that, was based in action, in pleasing oneself through work. There is the germ of a political programme in this formulation since to bring about the conditions under which it is possible for everyone's work to be 'hallowed' by art would require a social transformation.

Looked at from the confines of art historical practice, this understanding of the fine and decorative arts as forms of pleasurable work led Morris to conclude that the truest and most complete judgments about them had to be based on an assessment of the social conditions under which they were made. Morris was a strong supporter of what in the days before the 'new art history' used to be called the social history of art, the premises of which he sets out in the 1884 address to the Society for the Protection of Ancient Buildings (SPAB), 'Architecture and History'. Composed when the lessons of Marx's *Capital* were still new to him, it is one of his best works, packed full of energy and conviction, yet for all its breathless sincerity there is much of real and lasting value to Marxist cultural historians. The Morris we meet in it is an economic determinist, but not a crude one. He subjects the precious surface of art to analysis without destroying its beauty. There is no soulless dissection, no parsing of art into constituent vectors of signification.

Morris, then, promoted the idea of architecture as a form of feeling, and the intensity with which he put this idea across was exceptional, perhaps still is, among architectural writers. But how far did architecture extend? Did it stop at structure or was it confined to the ornamental side of high style building? Not being of a systematic cast of mind Morris sidestepped the issue by claiming that in an ideal world architecture would not even be considered as a subject in its own right. The very tendency to discuss it in isolation from the other applied arts and from life more generally had caused its decline. He preferred to treat architecture as a kind of shorthand for the totality of the man-made environment, and whenever Morris used the word he was only a few breaths away from issues outside of architecture as we normally think of it: environmental pollution, landscape conservation, consumer activism, advertising, public provision, transport and town planning. This totalizing vision must be borne firmly in mind if this collection of essays is to be of anything more than academic interest. The real reason for reading Morris on architecture is to see how a building is part of a larger complex of values. Morris's picture of architecture is one taken from the air. He moves effortlessly from the simplest terraced house, to the city of which it is part, and after that to the relationship between town and country, at each stage pausing to consider the social side of building and of the physical environment. This proneness always to drift means that no edition of his writings on architecture can ever be truly defin-itive, since many fine passages treating the subject are to be found in works which promise to be about something else.

And this brings me to what I see as Morris's most admirable quality as a thinker and cultural critic. He objected to the way in which modern capitalist economies broke down all experience and understanding into smaller and smaller units. The emer-gence of the modern profession of architecture (the Institute of British Architects was founded in the year of his birth, 1834) was a sign of a larger cultural process in which traditional human relations of community had been replaced by networks of social exchange. The tokens of this exchange, commodities, he found distasteful, shades of real experience, empty gestures. Our so-called post-Modern condition—'so-called' because Carlyle actually diagnosed it as early as 1843 in *Past and Present*—was to Morris a kind of hell. He could see no virtue in the instant and effortless transposition of cultural signs, of the incessant switches which rob things of their original meanings and uses. There is, in short, no way to square Morris with those critics today who preach redemption through the embrace of fragmented cultural icons. With a clear sense of moral preference, Morris called on his audience to overcome alienation by paying careful attention to those parts of the world which epitomized a once whole existence, the fine and decorative arts, literature, the unspoilt countryside, beautiful old buildings.

There were occasions, though, when Morris set himself the task of talking about architecture in its conventional sense, and when he did so he usually started with the definition Ruskin had set out at the start of *The Seven Lamps of Architecture* (1849), of architecture as distinguished from mere utilitarian building by the use of ornament.[4] 'The word Architecture,' he wrote in 1881, 'has, I suppose, to most of you the meaning of the art of building nobly and ornamentally.'

> But noble as that art is by itself, and though it is specially the art of civilisation, it neither ever has existed nor ever can exist alive and progressive by itself, but must cherish and be cherished by all the crafts ...
>
> It is this union of the arts, mutually helpful and harmoniously subordinated to one another, which I have learned to think of as Architecture, and when I use the word to-night, that is what I shall mean by it and nothing narrower.[5]

Eight years later he virtually repeats these words in the introduction to 'Gothic Architecture', but by this time his understanding of the relationship between art and life has deepened, leading him to conclude that the craft totality he is trying to describe has still wider social and spiritual significance. Architecture should ultimately be understood as 'man's expression of the value of life, and also the production of [works of architecture] makes his life of value ...' Architecture then is nothing less than the art of living well and nobly.

When speaking about the real world of buildings, this enlarged conception of architecture leads Morris to blur the distinction between polite architecture and the vernacular tradition. In his first public lecture, 'The Decorative Arts' (1877), Morris argued that all English medieval buildings, whatever their kind or size, sit beautifully in the landscape.

> ... at its best [English art] had an inventiveness, an individuality, that grander styles [i.e., classical architecture] have never overpassed; its best too, and that was in its very heart, was given as freely to the yeoman's house, and the humble village church, as to the lord's palace or the mighty cathedral... [a] sweet, natural and unaffected [art], an art of peasants rather than of merchant-princes or [of] courtiers ...[6]

Placing high and low on the same continuum got Morris into difficult territory, because although on this and other occasions he dignified unpretentious vernacular buildings by calling them architecture, he just as often spoke about architecture in a way which suggests it could not simply be craft. In *News from Nowhere* (published serially in 1890) the distinction between high and low still obtains. Ordinary dwellings are plain, quiet and unassuming; public buildings are highly ornamented. Morris never quite resolved the contradiction between his political commitment to the 'art of the people' and the deep personal attraction he felt for artistic achievement as conventionally understood.

Early Writings

Morris's intense love of medieval architecture is thought to have been formed in childhood. Sadly, though, there is very little primary evidence recording the nature of his youthful engagement with medieval building. Most of what is taken for fact can be traced back to late nineteenth-century sources. J.W. Mackail crossed this evidential gap in fine Vasarian style, observing simply that 'The love of the Middle Ages was born in him'.[7] At an early age Morris is said to have toured the Essex countryside near to his Woodford home in

search of fragments of Olde England, manor houses and
medieval parish churches mostly. At the age of eight and in the
company of his father, he visited Canterbury Cathedral and the
old Abbey at Minster in Thanet on the Isle of Sheppey. Mackail
relates how later in life Morris managed to describe the smallest
detail of the Abbey but he does not say exactly what this meant.
It might have been a detailed description or nothing more than a
rapid recitation of principal features. Nor does Mackail suggest
what to me seems likely, that Morris's memory had probably
been refreshed through his work on the committee of the SPAB.

A more detailed understanding of medieval architecture is
supposed to have been developed at Marlborough College, set in
a landscape rich in prehistoric and medieval remains. When
Morris was not travelling about the countryside in search of
tumuli or Perpendicular clerestories, he was cloistered in the
College library, 'well provided with works on archaeology and
ecclesiastical architecture'.[8] What books did he read? Only imagination can supply the bibliography. Certainly Marlborough
would have owned some of the eighteenth-century books on the
area's prehistoric remains, at the very least Richard Colt Hoare's
Ancient Wiltshire. It is also safe to assume Morris had read one
or more of the many taxonomies of medieval style, including
the first and most influential, Thomas Rickman's *Attempt to
Discriminate the Styles of English Architecture* ... (1817). Indeed this is
one of the few standard works on architecture he named in later
writings. Did he know something of the antiquarian tradition
which formed the background to Rickman? I have not
discovered anything to suggest a detailed appreciation, for when
he recounted the beginnings of the Revival he generally passed
over this important period choosing instead to see the work not
of scholars but of poets, in particular Blake, Byron, Coleridge,
Keats, Scott and Shelley, as initiating the movement.[9]

It is impossible, therefore, to see how Mackail was justified in
concluding that on leaving Marlborough, Morris 'knew most of

what there was to know about English Gothic'.[10] More than
Bloxam, Freeman, Neale, Petit, Pugin, or Willis, each a master of
the history of gothic architecture. This is pure boasting, for if
Morris really had developed such an advanced understanding of
medieval architecture as a young man we would expect some
evidence for it, an annotated itinerary or notes on reading, a book
filled with information on country churches, perhaps a few
sketches or maybe a brief article on some remote church for one
or another amateur society's annual proceedings. Instead there is
nothing. It is not even known when he first read Ruskin.

Fortunately as we approach the start of Morris's Oxford years
one figure stands out as most likely to have furnished him with
the opportunity of learning something of Gothic architecture,
the Rev. Frederick Barlow Guy. Assistant Master at the Forest
School near Walthamstow, Guy also tutored boys preparing for
university entry exams, which is how he came to work with
Morris for the best part of the year before he went up to Exeter
College in January 1853. Morris sat the Oxford matriculation
exam in June 1852, but stayed on for six months with Guy, ample
time for the study of subjects which would not normally have
been on the university syllabus. From what is known of Guy,
medieval architecture must have been one of them.[11] Guy's
father was vicar of Howden in the East Riding, and between 1840
and 1850 had made some attempt to restore the minster with its
splendid late fourteenth-century crossing tower. Guy was at
Lincoln College from about 1844 to 1847–8, and during those
years he was an active member of the Oxford Architectural
Society (OAS). Later he persuaded one of the part-time teachers
at the Forest School to join. The son of the School's owner, the
Rev. J.S. Gilderdale, was a student at Oriel and also a member. In
that summer of 1852 Guy took Morris and some other pupils on
a holiday to Alphington which featured a visit to the church at
Ottery St Mary, then newly restored and redecorated by the
architect William Butterfield under the auspices of the Exeter

Diocesan Architectural Society, a group with close links to both the OAS and the better known Cambridge Camden Society.

It has never been shown that Morris himself joined the OAS, but then that influential Society did not publish membership lists as assiduously as its sister group at Cambridge. Its papers survive only in fragmentary form at the Bodleian.[12] Still there is enough left to form a clear picture of its character. For a start the OAS was much less sectarian than the Cambridge Camden Society, and this may have influenced Morris whose understanding of medieval architecture as set down even in early writings is not restricted to the ecclesiological or High Church point of view. This openness was particularly apparent in a series of debates on church restoration mounted in the early 1840s.[13] In them Edward Augustus Freeman, better known for his later work on the Norman Conquest, called for a conservative approach to monuments care, one which anticipated the view put forward by the SPAB in several regards. The OAS actually oversaw the restoration of two ancient churches, Dorchester Abbey and Great Haseley Church.[14] Relative to the standards of the day these works were sensitive. All that can be said, then, is that Guy probably introduced Morris to Gothic architecture and put him in contact with the OAS. This in turn may explain why he entered into articles with G.E. Street (1824–81) in January 1856, since that architect was active in the Oxford Society.

So a path was open to Morris, but he does not seem to have taken it, since nothing in his later writings on architecture betrays a scholar's understanding. In 'The Gothic Revival', delivered in March 1884, there is a slightly shambolic overview of world architectural history which seems to have been cribbed hastily from James Fergusson's *A History of Architecture in All Countries* (1862–7).[15] The following year, in evidence before a parliamentary select committee, Morris tried to argue that a particular architectural feature was common but on questioning was unable to defend his claim.[16] And as for the detailed fabric reports he signed on behalf of the SPAB, these were usually written in committee with the help of expert advice or from published sources. His knowledge of medieval architecture was passive, that of a consumer of architectural histories not a writer of them.

In view of how little is known for sure of Morris's early exposure to architecture and architectural writing, three letters he wrote in 1855 recounting a journey to Normandy with Burne-Jones and William Fulford are most illuminating.[17] In one he judges the church at St Lo the finest he has seen because it was built 'almost uniformly in a style like our Early English, very plain but very beautiful'.[18] This observation was in step with recent developments in the Gothic Revival; in the early 1850s the preference for late thirteenth- and fourteenth-century Gothic as espoused by Pugin gave way to an appreciation of the austerity and structural lucidity of the early Gothic, ushering in the start of twenty years of architectural Primitivism. In general, though, the detailed notices of architecture contained in these letters are lifeless, even perfunctory, perhaps remembered with the help of Murray's *Hand-Book for Travellers in France* ... (the fifth edition of which appeared in 1854).[19] In these letters of 1855, notices of buildings seem always on the verge of tipping over into depictions of the countryside, which as pieces of writing clearly pleased Morris more than architectural descriptions.

A similar switching from architecture to nature occurs in Morris's 'The Story of the Unknown Church' published in the first number of the *Oxford and Cambridge Magazine* in January 1856. The medieval French abbey which provides the setting for this proto-Symbolist tale is beautiful less for its intrinsic architectural merits—the details of the building receive barely a mention—than for its setting, the great glory of which is the monk's garden with its poplars, trellised crimson roses, and hollyhocks, 'great spires of pink, orange, red and white'. The work of the master mason, the narrator, is interrupted by a vision. With his mallet poised to strike, time and place disappear in a flood of natural images. In this piece Morris aims to enter into the mind of the medieval craftsman, offering a practical demonstration of what Ruskin described in 'The Nature of Gothic'.

The clearest exposition of Morris's architectural agenda in his early years is to be found in an article which also appeared in the *Oxford and Cambridge Magazine* of 1856. 'The Churches of North France, No. 1, Shadows of Amiens' is not, by Morris's own admission, a cold analysis of the early Gothic as expressed in the Cathedral. It is his attempt to capture something of the passion he feels on seeing the building. Amiens engenders in him a frenzy, and he feels compelled, as if in a trance, to capture every nuance of its beauty, until the building itself, like the French landscape he wrote about in 1855, disappears under a wave of effusion. But before giving himself (and the reader) over to this reverie, he feels bound to offer a justification, to say precisely what it is he sees in Amiens and why it deserves such a treatment. He comes up with two very personal responses: the experience of 'remembering' which such magnificent buildings engender and the sensation of 'love' he feels in their presence.

Not long ago I saw for the first time some of the churches of North France; still more recently I saw them for the second time; and, remembering the love I have for them and the longing that was in me to see them, during the time that came between the first and second visit, I thought I should like to tell people of some of those things I felt when I was there;—there among those mighty tombs of the long-dead ages.

And I thought that even if I could say nothing else about these grand churches, I could at least tell men how much I loved them; so that, though they might laugh at me for my foolish and confused words, they might yet be moved to see what there was that made me speak my love, though I could give no reason for it.

For I will say here that I think those same churches of North France the grandest, the most beautiful, the kindest and most loving of all the buildings that the earth has ever borne; and, thinking of their past-away builders, can I see through them, very faintly, dimly, some little of the mediaeval times, else dead, and gone from me for ever,—voiceless for ever.

> And those same builders, still surely living, still real men, and
> capable of receiving love, I love no less than the great men, poets and
> painters and such like, who are on earth now, no less than my
> breathing friends whom I can see looking kindly on me now. Ah! do
> I not love them with just cause, who certainly loved me, thinking of
> me sometimes between the strokes of their chisels ...[20]

Throughout 'Amiens' Morris strains to express the idea that the
stones themselves are alive, as though the intimate physical contact between mason and stone imparted a real animistic charge.

'Amiens' is also unashamedly the work of a tourist. In
Morris's estimation the compressed experience of seeing a
building on a brief tour allows a visitor to grasp the power of its
artistry better than endless hours spent drawing and measuring,
which is just as well since he admits to having made no notes or
drawings during this visit, relying instead on reminiscence aided
with photographs.[21] Photographs liberated Morris's architectural
vision. With them safely packed away, he was free to experience
the sensations generated by the monument, and then later, un-
packing the images, to recall these emotions according to fancy,
enhancing the facts recorded there with what could be remembered in the mind's eye. Morris especially loved the lack of
colour in photographs, for their inferiority as surrogates en-
hanced his impressions. The gulf between printed image and the
building as remembered is necessarily so profound that the
original grows in power by comparison. Far from cheapening the
original, photographs by their very remove from reality increased
its value.

'Amiens' was published at the very moment Morris started in
the architectural office of G.E. Street, and it is surely significant
that that architect was himself then publishing a series of letters
on Gothic architecture outside England.[22] Street was a devoted
architectural tourist, much more so than Morris. The slightly
older man travelled incessantly, making special trips to the
continent nearly every summer of his adult life.[23] Back in
England he turned his notes and sketches to good professional

account by publishing many articles and two books on continental Gothic. The first of these, *Brick and Marble in the Middle
Ages. Notes of a Tour of North Italy* appeared in the same summer of
1855 that saw Morris in northern France. *Brick and Marble* was
the result of journeys undertaken since 1853, journeys inspired
by Ruskin's second volume of the *Stones of Venice*. Street's interest
in going to Italy was strictly professional. He wanted to test some
of Ruskin's assertions and in the process to treat Italian Gothic
as a kind of case study. The strong classical tradition in Italy
never quite yielded to the Gothic, or so the argument went, and
as a result Italian medieval architecture showed these contrary
principles (the classical horizontal versus the Gothic vertical) at
war with one another. Street concluded that the struggle had
ended in compromise to the detriment of architectural quality,
suggesting, by analogy with Victorian England where the propo-
nents of these two schools were themselves struggling, that only
pure Gothic would lead to a rational, structurally efficient
modern architecture.

The comparison between Street's writing on continental
Gothic and Morris's 'Amiens' is revealing. Street saw travel first
and last as a professional opportunity, whereas Morris went to the
continent for pleasure pure and simple: 'my two friends and I
have been in a state of ecstasy since we landed [in France]' was
how he described it to his mother in a letter written from Rouen
on 29 July 1855.[24] It was not that Street was blind to the beauty
of medieval buildings—there are many passages in *Brick and
Marble* which would sit well in a picturesque travel account—it
was just that he was single-minded. Street's fixation on the facts
of Gothic is at times truly wearying. He assessed every bit of
medieval architecture he set eyes on, even buildings seen in a
rapid whirl around a town between trains.

Is it asking too much of the twenty-one-year-old Morris to
have treated travel as a chance to broaden his architectural reper-
toire? Perhaps not, since there were examples of young men in

the same position whose intention in going abroad to look at architecture was nearer to Street's. Not long before Morris was in France, Norman Shaw and W.E. Nesfield were on the continent carefully studying the medieval buildings they found there. Shaw drew constantly; perspectives as well as carefully measured plans, elevations and sections. He does not seem to have had any plans to publish his work, but, as Andrew Saint has written, 'In his own mind, this extended tour was purely educational'.[25]

What could it have been, then, in view of their fundamentally different approaches to architecture, that drew Morris to Street, and why did Street, in his turn, go out of his way to encourage and then befriend[26] the dreamy and impractical young man who presented himself at his office in January 1856? We can only speculate about the older man's motivations, and it may be that Philip Webb, Street's principal assistant, served as an intermediary. In any case Morris's decision to enter into articles with Street was probably explained by their common interest in Ruskin, for as much as any architect then practising Street was eager to translate Ruskin's theories into practice.[27] Street pioneered the 'Muscular Gothic', the geometrically pure style informed by Ruskin's 'Lamp of Power', enhancing its primitivism with another 'Ruskinism', structural polychromy. (Street might have disapproved of Italian Gothic as style, but he admired the way its architects had used differently coloured building stones.) Street was also committed to improving the quality of the arts applied to building by studying craft techniques. He is said to have learned smithing in order to design the ironwork for his early masterpiece, All Saints at Boyne Hill in Maidenhead (begun in 1855), and then to have carried out some of the painting inside the church himself.

Apart from anything else, though, Morris's decision to enter Street's office showed terrific business judgment, for in professional terms everything about Street spelled financial success. He had finished his training with a distinguished architect, George

Gilbert Scott, and in 1850 was appointed Architect to the Diocese of Oxford. He left London[28] to be nearer his work in this large rural diocese, a risky step for a relative unknown to take but one which soon paid off. The bishop of Oxford, Samuel Wilberforce (1805–73), was committed to improving the architectural profile of the Church in his diocese, and Street was his sergeant-at-arms in all things architectural.[29]

When Street moved his office back to London in August 1856, Morris followed, but by this point his interests were beginning to shift. He attached himself to a new art, painting, and a new master, Dante Gabriel Rossetti. By the start of 1857 Morris's architectural career was over. With it went his desire to write about architecture in prose form, even though the work of Morris, Marshall, Faulkner and Co. (the decorative arts firm formed on 11 April 1861) brought him into close contact with medieval and modern buildings as well as with the leading architects of his generation. The exact reasons for his leaving Street's office are unrecorded, but two stories later recounted by one of Morris's closest friends, the architect Philip Webb, suggest that he was simply not suited to a no-nonsense profession. The first took place in Street's Oxford office in 1856. When set to draw a Romanesque doorway at St Augustine's Abbey in Canterbury, Morris is said to have 'suffered much tribulation in delineating the many arch mouldings', eventually destroying his drawing with the point of his compass.[30] Two years later, on a summer jaunt to look at French Gothic, Webb recalls leaving Morris on his own in the choir of Amiens Cathedral to make a drawing, taking to the gallery with the third member of their party, Charles Faulkner. After a few minutes Webb and Faulkner looked down to see how their friend was getting on. 'We saw him struggle with himself and suddenly go away—he had upset the ink bottle all over his drawing.'[31] What these anecdotes record about Morris's engagement with architecture is consistent with the temper revealed in his early writings where architecture is not seen to lie in superficial detail, in anything so simple and straightforward as design. Architecture is rather a matter of deeper meanings, ineffable perhaps, metaphysical almost certainly, and as such best understood by intuition. Reason simply does not enter into the equation, and drilling the point of his compass into the paper is a fine metaphor for Morris's Romantic yearning, for his desire to merge with the spirit pulsing beneath the skin of medieval matter. The lack of clarity sometimes met with in Morris's writing seems to me less the result of carelessness (although Morris could certainly be careless) than it does of frustration.

Although Morris gave up writing about architecture in detail in 1856, he most certainly did not lose interest in buildings, which make countless appearances in the poetry of his middle years. Perhaps the best known instance are the lines from the Prologue to *The Earthly Paradise* which puts in verse form his vision of London in the past which might well be confused with what he was to imagine for its future in *News from Nowhere*.

Why did Morris stop writing about architecture until spring 1877? Perhaps no explanation is needed, but given the intensity of his involvement in the last two decades of his life, it is odd that what he thought about architectural developments in these years has not come down to us. Or it may be that the building and decorating of Morris's Red House at Bexleyheath (1859–60) and the subsequent work of Morris, Marshall, Faulkner and Co. should be understood as his attempt to put these early theories into practice.

Arguably Kelmscott Manor, the luscious late medieval house by the headwaters of the Thames in rural Oxfordshire (plate 1), urged him to take up his pen once more in the cause of architecture. A letter to Charles Faulkner in spring 1871 records the excitement Morris felt at the prospect of living there.[32] He took the lease jointly with Rossetti and then left for Iceland. The strain on his relationship with his wife and Rossetti's presence in the house prevented this architectural idyll from taking possession of his imagination all at once. Still, the increasingly regular journeys between sordid, filthy London and the dreamy purity of Kelmscott set him thinking about the place of architecture in modern life.[33] In 1874, the year which saw Rossetti's final departure from Kelmscott and the tumultuous reorganization of the firm, these stray observations begin to coalesce into an architectural programme.[34]

Mature Writings

Morris's work for the Society for the Protection of Ancient Buildings, the first pressure group dedicated explicitly to the conservation of old buildings (and therefore opposed not merely to demolitions but also to harsh restorations), was what finally tipped the balance. A letter Morris wrote to the *Athenaeum* on 5 March 1877 got the whole thing going, and for the next five years he spent endless hours establishing a casework protocol and a sound financial basis, allowing the Society to continue into the new century and up to the present day. As its founder and most prominent member Morris had no choice but to put the case for 'Protection' in writing, so in a sense he was forced to commit his thoughts on architecture to words.

The Manifesto of the SPAB was the first fruit of Morris's renewed engagement with architecture. Although there is a great deal of interest in it to conservationists, the bulk of the text is in fact taken up with an attack on the Gothic Revival, in Morris's eyes one of the greatest catastrophes to befall mankind since the Black Death. By promulgating the view that history had a fixed shape and pattern, rules to be mastered and then applied, the Revival had killed the art of architecture. Measured drawings and precise quantities had smothered the last traces of creative industry, reducing architecture to the assemblage of standardised kit parts as set out in one of the many handbooks of style. Even worse than this was the havoc that the profession was wreaking on real examples of medieval building art. The craze for church restoration, fueled partly by the Gothic Revival and partly by the liturgical revival within the Church of England, had led to the destruction of all that was authentic and poetic about medieval churches. Morris was old enough to remember the days when most of the churches met with on a country tour were ramshackle and decayed, perfect subjects for the picturesque viewmaker. By the 1870s untouched medieval buildings were increasingly hard to find. They had become an endangered species.[35]

The Manifesto is clear about the problem but it offers no solution or even much in the way of palliative care. In late April, several weeks after composing it, Morris argued that the best course of action was to suspend all works of restoration until it could be decided whether the Gothic experiment had succeeded in creating a vital contemporary style.[36] If the Revivalists carried the day, then Morris promised to withdraw his objections. The 'we-have-reached-the-end-of-history-and-can-do-nothing-original' critique did not serve the interests of his new Society well for two reasons. First, ancient fabrics were known to fail from time to time, and, second, this line of argument was insulting to professional architects, the one group most likely to realize the Society's ideal of conservative, gentle repair. Morris, who deserves more credit for pragmatism than he is usually given, soon eased his critique of the Revival, and then, slowly, came around to endorsing it as the starting point for a genuine modern architecture—so long, of course, as Gothic Revival architects agreed not to impose their own notions of what was right and proper on medieval buildings.

'The Prospects of Architecture in Civilisation' (1881) offers the conditions under which this hoped-for modern architecture might flourish. Architecture should no longer be 'an esoteric mystery shared by a little band of superior beings', that is, architects. It must be democratized by being brought into line with the natural world after the example of traditional English buildings. Professional interest in the vernacular was by this point well established[37] (and would by the close of the decade be reinvigorated by a new generation of architects[38]) but Morris stops just short of advocating copyism. The way around this impasse will become clear once social conditions have improved. There is the barest hint that some form of public ownership is required, land nationalization perhaps, but Morris never fully embraced the state. In the meantime the only viable course of action was to guard old buildings and the unspoiled parts of the countryside by protest, and to try to emulate the unpretentious, quiet qualities of vernacular building, an agenda set out in his 1881 lecture 'Art and the Beauty of the Earth'.[39] In these years, from 1876 to 1883, Morris believed it possible to bring about far-reaching social changes from the top down, by revolutionizing the ideological superstructure of capitalist society. This Morris, the one of 'The Prospects of Architecture in Civilisation', always appealed more to the membership of the SPAB—who were willing to see England transformed by a kind of radicalized consumerism—than did the strictly Marxist Morris of the mid-1880s, whose view on architecture is most clearly and forcefully delineated in 'Architecture and History' of 1884.[40]

As the 1880s wore on Morris's position on the Gothic Revival noticeably softened, and before very long he was back to seeing it as the first step towards a new architecture, with some reservations of course. In the 'Gothic Revival' of 1884 he defended the pointed styles as the most structurally sound and efficient then in use.[41] In 'The Revival of Architecture' of 1888 Morris praised the Revival as a kind of Gothic renaissance, admirable for having taken up the 'link of historical art where the pedants of the so-called renaissance had dropped it'. He is convinced 'that the medieval style was capable of new life and fresh development' by virtue of its 'marvellous elasticity'. In 'Gothic Architecture' of 1889 Morris finally gave in, taking a position against classicism alongside the very Goths he had attacked in the SPAB Manifesto. Morris left us with a good idea of his own architectural tastes during this period, and here too there are signs of movement. As late as 1880 he expressed admiration for new work which was based on simple, solidly built forms rather than ornamental elaboration, in other words the vigorously primitive brick churches which Street, George Frederick Bodley (1827–1907), and William Burges (1827–81) had started to design in the early 1850s. In this regard he is close to endorsing Charles Eastlake's conclusions about recent architecture as put forth in his widely read *History of the Gothic Revival* of 1872. By 1884 Morris's opinion was shifting in line with changes in the work of some of those same architects he had known as a young man. By the late 1860s Bodley and a handful of church architects were beginning to use the forms and details of fourteenth- and fifteenth-century Gothic with considerable skill. This highly refined and ornate style had previously been dismissed by critics as being too effete to stand the strain of rigorous development, but soon its sheer elegance won out over theories of architectural style. In 'The Gothic Revival' Morris recalled a visit 'some four years ago' to a church built by a friend of his. Looking into the richly carved chancel, partly shrouded in late afternoon light, Morris admitted to feelings he had only ever had in the presence of real medieval buildings. Close inspection of the carvings brought him rudely back to the present, since here the stink of capitalism showed itself in harsh, mechanical workmanship.[42] Morris never gave more fulsome praise to a modern building, and it is maddening that there are no further clues to help make an identification. My best guess is that he was writing about Bodley's splendid church at Hoar Cross, largely complete by April 1876 (plate 2).

Unfortunately, Morris only ever named his favourite modern buildings once, in 'The Revival of Architecture' of 1888. The list will come as no surprise to those familiar with Victorian architecture: E.R. Robson's buildings for the London School Board, presumably the early works of 1870–75 because by the mid-1880s School Board design had hit a fallow period (plate 3); Bodley's new buildings at Magdalen College flanking the old Grammar Hall of c1480, that is, St Swithun's Buildings of 1880–84 and the President's Lodgings of 1886–8 (plate 4); Norman Shaw's Chelsea Houses, some of which were built for people in touch with the Morris circle and active in the SPAB (plate 5); and G.E. Street's Royal Courts of Justice in the Strand, of 1874 to 1882 (plate 6). In Morris's estimation this last was the finest public building in London, being both 'reasonable' and 'beautiful'.

However, the buildings Morris loved best were medieval (plate 7). The choir of Westminster Abbey, built around 1250, was to him perfect architecture. This was the nearest Morris ever came to saying he preferred French to English Gothic, for the Abbey's choir resembles Amiens, Reims and Sainte Chapelle more than most English buildings of similar stature and date. Otherwise his tastes were strongly nationalistic.

Morris was of two minds when it came to English architecture derived from the southern European classical tradition. In lectures he usually defamed it, taking a lead from Gothic Revival theorists and architects; however, under Morris's stewardship, the SPAB led the way in the appreciation of the architecture of Wren and the Wren School, mounting an effective campaign to protect the City of London churches from sale and demolition. In 1879 Morris managed to persuade the Metropolitan Board of Works in London to repair York Water Gate (erected in 1626 to give access to the Duke of Buckingham's mansion).[43] Two years later Morris tried to prevent the widening of Magdalen Bridge (plate 8) in Oxford. Although this campaign, one of his most passionate for the Society, was fought on the grounds of what is today know as 'townscape value', Morris discerned a 'naif classicality' in the architecture of the bridge which was in his estimation not entirely 'un-Gothic'.[44]

Morris always had difficulty with architecture from the time of William III and Queen Anne, and in effect damned it with faint praise, claiming that it was good only to the extent it possessed 'some feeling of the Gothic'.[45] Ultimately, though, it failed as any product of 'the workshop and division of labour' must, for it came from 'a period when all that was left of the craft guilds was the corruption of them'. Standing on its own this judgment was bound to insult the architects of his generation who were committed to reviving the style of Queen Anne, including his early SPAB ally John James Stevenson (1831–1908). Morris gave in, grudgingly, out of politeness perhaps, and one can almost hear the sigh of condescension in the sympathy he expresses for the architects of his day who, working in a time of limited expectations, should be forgiven for designing in a way which was suited to the conditions of modern building. At least late seventeenth- and early eighteenth-century brick stood up to the London atmosphere, and at least it did not upset the leafy elegance of a typical village green, but then in Morris's view even a house of the 1760s, if surrounded by trees and a well planted garden, had the potential to be handsome.[46]

Morris is almost at his best when he writes about architecture he hates, the architecture of the modern town as epitomized by London's terraced houses and villas of the late eighteenth century to his own day, the very buildings excised from paradise in *News from Nowhere*. In London commercial interests and architectural meanness had conspired to produce the most dismal and inhumane streetscapes imaginable. In 1877 he lamented the unbearable flatness and regularity of the capital's streets.[47] In 1878, debating the merits of which bit of town he should move his family to, he snarled over the Regency stucco of St John's Wood and John Nash's Regent's Park.[48] In 1884 Bloomsbury's Gower Street (begun in 1790), just around the corner from his

Queen Square premises, was held up as the paradigm of all that was wrong with late Georgian building[49] (plate 9). The mass-produced classicism of Victoria's middle years, heir to rows of slate lidded Georgian brick boxes, faired little better. Notting Hill, Holland Park and Bayswater he simply could not take[50] (plate 10). Morris was disgusted less by their outward appearance, though that was bad enough, than his perception of them as creatures of fickle taste, social niceties, and commerce, occupying land once covered with fine old buildings and handsome parks. The 'enemy', he told an audience in 1889, was the suburb, the ceaseless multiplication of the 'middle class terraced house' in all its various forms.[51]

It is a bleak prospect, and the reader who despairs before it should be forgiven. Remarkably, though, Morris himself almost always managed to end on an upbeat note, and this is usually just enough to carry most readers along with him. He is at his gloomiest in the First and Second Annual Addresses to the SPAB, and not surprisingly since two years of hard work had produced, at most, two or three successes for the fledgling pressure group.[52] However, the concluding section of 'The Art of the People' (1879) finds Morris in better spirits.[53] To speak out against an evil, he told his audience, at least heralds the start of its undoing. The same point comes up at the close of 'The Revival of Architecture' nine years later. Here, in the conclusion to his lecture, Morris's skill as a polemicist shows itself, for it is never easy to rally the troops in the face of an overwhelming onslaught. Somehow he manages to keep alarmism and cock-eyed optimism equally at arm's length.

What, then, is Morris's value as an architectural thinker? I take it for granted that, being widely regarded in his own day as an innovator, what he had to say is of interest to students of Victorian cultural history generally. Obviously his writings will be important to thinkers on the Left, since Morris explored the limits not simply of social realism in the visual and plastic arts but also of the social history of art. More than this is hard to say, since it is possible to make out at least two distinct Morrises in his architectural writings. The one who appears in 'The Prospects of Architecture' (1881), although upset by prevailing social order, still believes it possible to make a difference by taking informed choices about the way money is spent. The Morris of 'Architecture and History', written just three years later, denies that paradise can be achieved by carefully calculated, morally-sound purchases. Commodities are by their nature evil and dehumanizing. From time to time an architect or artist of genius might achieve a work of real beauty despite the squalid conditions of modern life, and his or her work might, in turn, suggest what art and life might be like after the revolution. So, apart from a handful of successful experiments, architecture is doomed until such time as society is reconstituted along fairer lines. In the meantime, the particular look of a house or a church or a meeting hall hardly mattered.

Notes

1   *Pioneers of Modern Design. From William Morris to Walter Gropius* (London: Faber and Faber, 1936). Pp. 21-7, 1975 edition (London: Penguin Books).

2   'The Nature of Gothic, and herein of the True Functions of the Workman in Art', reprinted in M. Morris (ed.), *William Morris: Artist, Writer, Socialist* (2 vols, Oxford: Basil Blackwell, 1936), I, pp. 292-5.

3   M. Swenarton, *Artisans and Architects. The Ruskinian Tradition in Architectural Thought* (London: Macmillan, 1989), pp. 61-95, at pp. 72-3.

4   J. Ruskin, *The Seven Lamps of Architecture* (Orpington, Kent: George Allen, 1880), p. 8.

5   'The Prospects of Architecture in Civilisation', in W. Morris, *Hopes and Fears for Art* (London: Ellis and White, 1882), p. 169 (p. 64 in this volume).

6   M. Morris (ed.), *The Collected Works of William Morris* (24 vols, London: Longman, Green & Co., 1910–15), XXII, pp. 3-27, at p. 18.

7   J.W. Mackail, *The Life and Work of William Morris* (2 vols, London: Longmans, 1899), I, p. 10.

8   Mackail, *The Life of William Morris*, I, p. 16.

9 'The Gothic Revival', [Parts I and II], reprinted in E. LeMire (ed.), *The Unpublished Lectures of William Morris* (Detroit: Wayne State University Press, 1969), pp. 72-5.

10 Mackail, *The Life of William Morris*, I, p. 16.

11 Ray Watkinson to author, 16 and 17 October 1995.

12 MSS. Dep.d.538, Bodleian Library, Oxford University.

13 *Reports of the OAS*, 12 and 26 May, and 9 June, 1841.

14 OAS *Reports*, 1847. Also MSS. Dep.d.540, Bodleian.

15 LeMire (ed.), *Unpublished Lectures*, pp. 57-64.

16 'Report with Proceedings of the Select Committee on the Restoration of Westminster Hall', *Parliamentary Papers*, 1884-5, vol. 13, pp. 89-92.

17 N. Kelvin (ed.), *The Collected Letters of William Morris* (4 vols, Princeton, NJ: Princeton University Press, 1984-96), I, pp. 16-22. 29 July, 7 and 10 August.

18 Kelvin, *Collected Letters*, I, pp. 18-19.

19 J.G. Links, *The Ruskins in Normandy. A Tour in 1848 with Murray's Handbook* (London: John Murray, 1968).

20 Reprinted in *Prose and Poetry by William Morris, 1856-1870* (London: Oxford University Press, 1920), pp. 617-31, at p. 617.

21 *Prose and Poetry by William Morris*, pp. 621-3.

22 *Ecclesiologist*, 1854, pp. 381-6; *Ecclesiologist*, 1855, pp. 21-36, pp. 361-73; 1858, pp. 362-72.

23 See D. Brownlee, *The Law Courts. The Architecture of G.E. Street* (Cambridge, MA: MIT Press, 1984), pp. 17-35.

24 Kelvin (ed.), *Collected Letters*, I, p. 17.

25 A. Saint, *Richard Norman Shaw* (London and New Haven: Yale University Press, 1976), p. 9.

26 W.R. Lethaby, *Philip Webb and His Work* (London: Oxford University Press, 1935), p. 20.

27 *Ecclesiologist*, 1852, pp. 237-62 and *An Urgent Plea for the Revival of the True Principles of Architecture in the Public Buildings of the University of Oxford*, (1853).

28 First for Wantage. He moved to Beaumont Street in Oxford in 1852.

29 C. Miele, 'The Gothic Revival and Gothic Architecture. The Restoration of Medieval Churches in Victorian Britain' (Ph.D. thesis, Institute of Fine Arts, New York University), pp. 342-7.

30 Lethaby, *Philip Webb*, pp. 15-6.

31 Lethaby, *Philip Webb*, p. 23.

32 Kelvin (ed.), *Collected Letters*, I, pp. 133-4. Kelvin dates this to 17 May.

33 Kelvin (ed.), *Collected Letters*, I, pp. 164-7. 8 and 24 October 1872.

34 Kelvin (ed.), *Collected Letters*, I, p. 218. 26 March 1874.

35 'Survey of Church Building and Restoration. 1840–1875', *Parliamentary Accounts and Papers*, LVIII, pp. 1-189, 1876.

36 Kelvin (ed.), *Collected Letters*, I, p. 362.

37 Saint, *Richard Norman Shaw*, pp. 24-36.

38 A. Crawford, *A Tour of Chipping Camden and Broadway* (London: The Victorian Society, 1978), pp. 1-5.

39 Morris (ed.), *Collected Works*, XXII, pp. 155-74.

40 C. Miele, '"A Small Knot of Cultivated People". William Morris and the Ideologies of Protection', *Art Journal*, Summer 1995, pp. 73-9.

41 LeMire (ed.), *Unpublished Lectures*, pp. 54-93, particularly pp. 55, 77.

42 LeMire (ed.), *Unpublished Lectures*, p. 83.

43 Kelvin (ed.), *Collected Letters*, I, pp. 570-1.

44 Kelvin (ed.), *Collected Letters*, II, pp. 55-6.

45 'The Revival of Architecture', in Morris (ed.), *Collected Works*, XXII, pp. 318-30, at p. 327. See also p. 136 in this volume.

46 W. Morris, *Hopes and Fears for Art* (London, Ellis and White, 1882) pp. 118-9

47 Kelvin (ed.), *Collected Letters*, I, p. 375.

48 Kelvin (ed.), *Collected Letters*, I, pp. 466-7.

49 LeMire (ed.), *Unpublished Lectures*, pp. 68-70.

50 Kelvin (ed.), *Collected Letters*, I, p. 459.

51 'The Arts and Crafts Today', 1889, reprinted in Morris (ed.), *Collected Works*, XXII, pp. 360-2.

52 C. Miele, 'The First Conservation Militants', in M. Hunter (ed.), *Preserving the Past* (London: Alan Sutton, 1996), pp. 17-37.

53 Morris, *Hopes and Fears for Art*, pp. 69 and 76-7.

NOTES ON TEXTS

'The Story of the Unknown Church': from *Prose and Poetry by William Morris, 1856–1870* (London: Oxford University Press, 1920), pp. 3-12. First published in *The Oxford and Cambridge Magazine*, I (January 1856), pp. 28-33.

'Manifesto of the Society for the Protection of Ancient Buildings': from N. Kelvin (ed.), *The Collected Letters of William Morris* (4 vols, Princeton, NJ: Princeton University Press, 1984–96), I, note on pp. 359-60.

'Address to the First Annual General Meeting of the Society for the Protection of Ancient Buildings': from *First Annual Report of the Committee of* the Society for the Protection of Ancient Buildings (1878), pp 7-16.

'The Prospects of Architecture in Civilisation': from W. Morris, *Hopes and Fears for Art* (London: Ellis and White, 1882), pp. 169-217.

'Architecture and History': from *Seventh Annual Report of the Society for the Protection of Ancient Buildings* (1884), pp. 49-76.

'The Housing of the Poor': from *Justice*, I, no. 27 (July 1884), pp. 4-5.

'The Revival of Architecture': from M. Morris (ed.), *The Collected Works of William Morris* (24 vols, London: Longman, Green & Co., 1910-15), XXII, pp. 318-30.

'Ugly London': from *The Pall Mall Gazette*, 48 (4 September 1888), pp. 1-2. Morris wrote this in response to a short notice in the journal's previous number (30 August, p. 11).

Extracts from 'Gothic Architecture': from M. Morris (ed.),

William Morris: Artist, Writer, Socialist (2 vols, Oxford: Basil Blackwell, 1936), I, pp. 266-86. First delivered as a lecture at the New Gallery of the Arts and Crafts Exhibition Society on 7 November 1889.

'The Influence of Building Materials upon Architecture': from Morris (ed.), *Collected Works*, XXII, pp. 391-405. First delivered at 20 November 1891.

Correspondence

Letter to the Editor of *The Athenaeum*: from Kelvin (ed.), *Collected Letters*, I, pp. 351-2. Printed in *The Athenaeum* for 10 March 1877.

Letter to *The Times* concerning the Destruction of the City of London Churches: from Kelvin (ed.), *Collected Letters*, I, pp. 477-8.

Letter to *The Daily News* against the Proposed Restoration of the West Front of San Marco in Venice: from Kelvin (ed.), *Collected Letters*, I, pp. 528-30.

PLATES

Plate 1 Kelmscott Manor, Oxon. Late sixteenth to late seventeenth centuries. Photograph taken in 1964, before Donald Insall's scheme of repairs. RCHME © Crown Copyright.

Plate 2 Church of the Holy Angels, Hoar Cross, Staffs. By G.F. Bodley, the main body of the church completed by 1876. RCHME © Crown Copyright.

Plate 3 West Street School, London Fields, Hackney. 1872–3 by E.R. Robson for the London School Board. This illustration from Robson's *School Architecture* of 1874. Copyright: Author.

Plate 4 Magdalen College, Oxford. The late medieval Grammar Hall in the centre with Bodley's St Swithun's Buildings of 1880–4 to the left and his President's Lodgings of 1886–8 to the right. Photograph taken in 1903. RCHME © Crown Copyright.

Plate 5 Swan House, Chelsea Embankment, Royal Borough of Kensington and Chelsea, London. 1875–7. Richard Norman Shaw for Wickham Flower (a SPAB member). The interior originally had some decorations by Morris and Co. Photograph taken in 1889. RCHME © Crown Copyright.

Plate 6 The Royal Courts of Justice in the Strand, 1874–82, designed by G.E. Street. RCHME © Crown Copyright.

Plate 7 Church of St John the Baptist, Inglesham, Wilts. Largely thirteenth century. The repairs begun in 1887 were paid for largely by the SPAB. Morris made several anonymous donations and visited the building several times while it was being repaired by the architect J.T. Micklethwaite. The first phase of works was completed by 1892. RCHME © Crown Copyright.

Plate 8 View of Magdalen College, Oxford, with John Gwynn's bridge of 1772–82 in the foreground. The subject of a SPAB campaign in 1881. Widened in 1882 to accommodate a tram line. Copyright: Oxford County Libraries.

Plate 9 Houses in Gower Street, nos. 87–97, London Borough of Camden. The street was developed in the 1790s. Photograph taken in 1943. RCHME © Crown Copyright.

Plate 10 House in Holland Park, c1865, built and developed by Francis and William Radford. In Morris's view the epitome of mid-Victorian bourgeois pretence. Copyright: Greater London History Library, Corporation of London.

ESSAYS AND ADDRESSES

THE STORY OF THE UNKNOWN CHURCH

1856

I was the master-mason of a church that was built more than six hundred years ago; it is now two hundred years since that church vanished from the face of the earth; it was destroyed utterly,—no fragment of it was left; not even the great pillars that bore up the tower at the cross, where the choir used to join the nave. No one knows now even where it stood, only in this very autumn-tide, if you knew the place, you would see the heaps made by the earth-covered ruins heaving the yellow corn into glorious waves, so that the place where my church used to be is as beautiful now as when it stood in all its splendour. I do not remember very much about the land where my church was; I have quite forgotten the name of it, but I know it was very beautiful, and even now, while I am thinking of it, comes a flood of old memories, and I almost seem to see it again,—that old beautiful land! only dimly do I see it in spring and summer and winter, but I see it in autumn-tide clearly now; yes, clearer, clearer, oh! so bright and glorious! yet it was beautiful too in spring, when the brown earth began to grow green: beautiful in summer, when the blue sky looked so much bluer, if you could hem a piece of it in between the new white carving; beautiful in the solemn starry nights, so solemn that it almost reached agony—the awe and joy one had in their great beauty. But of all these beautiful times, I remember the whole only of autumn-tide; the others come in bits to me; I can think only of parts of them, but all of autumn; and of all days and nights in autumn, I remember one more particularly. That autumn day the church was nearly finished, and the monks, for whom we were building the church, and the people, who lived in the town hard by, crowded round us oftentimes to watch us carving.

Now the great Church, and the buildings of the Abbey where the monks lived, were about three miles from the town, and the town stood on a hill overlooking the rich autumn country: it was girt about with great walls that had overhanging battlements, and towers at certain places all along the walls, and often we could see from the churchyard or the Abbey garden, the flash of helmets and spears, and the dim shadowy waving of banners, as the knights and lords and men-at-arms passed to and fro along the battlements; and we could see too in the town the three spires of the three churches; and the spire of the Cathedral, which was the tallest of the three, was gilt all over with gold, and always at night-time a great lamp shone from it that hung in the spire midway between the roof of the church and the cross at the top of the spire. The Abbey where we built the Church was not girt by stone walls, but by a circle of poplar trees, and whenever a wind passed over them, were it ever so little a breath, it set them all a-ripple; and when the wind was high, they bowed and swayed very low, and the wind, as it lifted the leaves, showed their silvery white sides, or as again in the lulls of it, it let them drop, kept on changing the trees from green to white, and white to green; moreover, through the boughs and trunks of the poplars, we caught glimpses of the great golden corn sea, waving, waving, waving for leagues and leagues; and among the corn grew burning scarlet poppies, and blue corn-flowers; and the corn-flowers were so blue, that they gleamed, and seemed to burn with a steady light, as they grew beside the poppies among the gold of the wheat. Through the corn sea ran a blue river, and always green meadows and lines of tall poplars followed its windings. The old Church had been burned, and that was the reason why the monks caused me to build the new one; the buildings of the Abbey were built at the same time as the burned-down Church, more than a hundred years before I was born, and they were on the north side of the Church, and joined to it by a cloister of round arches, and in the midst of the cloister was a lawn, and in the midst of that lawn, a fountain of marble, carved round about with flowers and strange beasts; and at the edge of the lawn, near the round arches, were a great many sun-flowers that were all in blossom on that autumn day; and up many of the pillars of the cloister crept passion-flowers and roses. Then farther from the Church, and past the cloister and its buildings, were many detached buildings, and a great garden round them, all within the circle of the poplar trees; in the garden were trellises covered over with roses, and convolvulus, and the great-leaved fiery nasturtium; and specially all along by the poplar trees were there trellises, but on these grew nothing but deep crimson roses; the hollyhocks too were all out in blossom at that time, great spires of pink, and orange, and red, and white, with their soft, downy leaves. I said that nothing grew on the trellises by the poplars but crimson roses, but I was not quite right, for in many places the wild flowers had crept into the garden from without; lush green briony, with green-white blossoms, that grows so fast, one could almost think that we see it grow, and deadly night-shade, La bella donna, O! so beautiful; red berry, and purple, yellow-spiked flower, and deadly, cruel-looking, dark green leaf, all growing together in the glorious days of early autumn. And in the midst of the great garden was a conduit, with its sides carved with histories from the Bible, and there was on it too, as on the fountain in the cloister, much carving of flowers and strange beasts. Now the Church itself was surrounded on every side but the north by the cemetery, and there were many graves there, both of monks and of laymen, and often the friends of those, whose bodies lay there, had planted flowers about the graves of those they loved. I remember one such particularly, for at the head of it was a cross of carved wood, and at the foot of it, facing the cross, three tall sun-flowers; then in the midst of the cemetery was a cross of stone, carved on one side with the Crucifixion of our Lord Jesus Christ, and on the other with Our Lady holding the Divine Child. So that day, that I specially remember, in Autumn-tide, when the church was nearly finished, I was carving in the central porch of the west front; (for I carved all those bas-reliefs in the west front with my own hand;) beneath me my sister Margaret was carving at the flower-work, and the little quatrefoils that carry the signs of the zodiac and emblems of the months: now my sister Margaret was rather more than twenty years old at that time, and she was very beautiful, with dark brown hair and deep calm violet eyes. I had lived with her all my life, lived with her almost alone latterly, for our father and mother died when she was quite young, and I loved her very much, though I was not thinking of her just then, as she stood beneath me carving. Now the central porch was carved with a bas-relief of the Last Judgement, and it was divided into three parts by horizontal bands of deep flower-work. In the lowest division, just over the doors, was carved The Rising of the Dead; above were angels blowing long trumpets, and Michael the Archangel weighing the souls, and the blessed led into heaven by angels, and the lost into hell by the devil; and in the topmost division was the Judge of the world.

All the figures in the porch were finished except one, and I remember when I woke that morning my exultation at the thought of my Church being so nearly finished; I remember, too, how a kind of misgiving mingled with the exultation, which, try all I could, I was unable to shake off; I thought then it was a rebuke for my pride, well, perhaps it was. The figure I had to carve was Abraham, sitting with a blossoming tree on each side of him, holding in his two hands the corners of his great robe, so that it made a mighty fold, wherein, with their hands crossed over their breasts, were the souls of the faithful, of whom he was called Father: I stood on the scaffolding for some time, while Margaret's chisel worked on bravely down below. I took mine in my hand, and stood so, listening to the noise of the masons inside, and two monks of the Abbey came and stood below me, and a knight, holding his little daughter by the hand, who every now and then looked up to him, and asked him strange questions. I did not think of these long, but began to think of Abraham, yet I could not think of him sitting there, quiet and solemn, while the Judgement-Trumpet was being blown; I rather thought of him as he looked when he chased those kings so far; riding far ahead of any of his company, with his mail-hood off his head, and lying in grim folds down his back, with the strong west wind blowing his wild black hair far out behind him, with the wind rippling the long scarlet pennon of his lance; riding there amid the rocks and the sands alone; with the last gleam of the armour of the beaten kings disappearing behind the winding of the pass; with his company a long, long way behind, quite out of sight, though their trumpets sounded faintly among the clefts of the rocks; and so I thought I saw him, till in his fierce chase he leapt, horse and man, into a deep river, quiet, swift and smooth; and there was something in the moving of the water-lilies as the breast of the horse swept them aside, that suddenly took away the thought of Abraham and brought a strange dream of lands I had never seen; and the first was of a place where I was quite alone, standing by the side of a river, and there was the sound of singing a very long way off, but no living thing of any kind could be seen, and the land was quite flat, quite without hills, and quite without trees too, and the river wound very much, making all kinds of quaint curves, and on the side where I stood there grew nothing but long grass, but on the other side grew, quite on to the horizon, a great sea of red corn-poppies, only paths of white lilies wound all among them, with here and there a great golden sun-flower. So I looked down at the river by my feet, and saw how blue it was, and how, as the stream went swiftly by, it swayed to and fro the long green weeds, and I stood and looked at the river for long, till at last I felt some one touch me on the shoulder, and, looking round, I saw standing by me my friend Amyot, whom I love better than any one else in the world, but I thought in my dream that I was frightened when I saw him, for his face had changed so, it was so bright and almost transparent, and his eyes gleamed and shone as I had never seen them do before. Oh! he was so wondrously beautiful, so fearfully beautiful! and as I looked at him the distant music swelled, and seemed to come close up to me, and then swept by us, and fainted away, at last died off entirely; and then I felt sick at heart, and faint, and parched, and I stooped to drink of the water of the river, and as soon as the water touched my lips, lo! the river vanished, and the flat country with its poppies and lilies, and I dreamed that I was in a boat by myself again, floating in an almost land-locked bay of the northern sea, under a cliffe of dark basalt. I was lying on my back in the boat, looking up at the intensely blue sky, and a long low swell from the outer sea lifted the boat up and let it fall again and carried it gradually nearer and nearer towards the dark cliff; and as I moved on, I saw at last, on the top of the cliff, a castle, with many towers, and on the highest tower of the castle there was a great white banner floating, with a red chevron on it, and three golden stars on the chevron; presently I saw too on one of the towers, growing in a cranny of the worn stones, a great bunch of golden and blood-red wall-flowers, and I watched the wall-flowers and banner for long; when suddenly I heard a trumpet blow from the castle, and saw a rush of armed men on to the battlements, and there was a fierce fight, till at last it was ended, and one went to the banner and pulled it down, and cast it over the cliff into the sea, and it came down in long sweeps, with the wind making little ripples in it;—slowly, slowly it came, till at last it fell over me and covered me from my feet till over my breast, and I let it stay there and looked again at the castle, and then I saw that there was an amber-coloured banner floating over the castle in place of the red chevron, and it was much larger than the other: also now, a man stood on the battlements, looking towards me; he had a tilting helmet on, with the visor down, and an amber-coloured surcoat over his armour: his right hand was ungauntletted, and he held it high above his head, and in his hand was the bunch of wall-flowers that I had seen growing on the wall; and his hand was white and small, like a woman's, for in my dream I could see even very far off things much clearer than we see real material things on the earth: presently he threw the wall-flowers over the cliff, and they fell in the boat just behind my head, and then I saw, looking down from the battlements of the castle, Amyot. He looked down towards me very sorrowfully, I thought, but, even as in the other dream, said nothing; so I thought in my dream that I wept for very pity, and for love of him, for he looked as a man just risen from a long illness, and who will carry till he dies a dull pain about with him. He was very thin, and his long black hair drooped all about his face, as he leaned over the battlements looking at me: he was quite pale, and his cheeks were hollow, but his eyes large, and soft, and sad. So I reached out my arms to him, and suddenly I was walking with him in a lovely garden, and we said nothing, for the music which I had heard at first was sounding close to us now, and there were many birds in the boughs of the trees: oh, such birds! gold and ruby, and emerald, but they sung not at all, but were quite silent, as though they too were listening to the music. Now all this time Amyot and I had been looking at each other, but just then I turned my head away from him, and as soon as I did so, the music ended with a long wail, and when I turned again Amyot was gone; then I felt even more sad and sick at heart than I had before when I was by the river, and I leaned against a tree, and put my hands before my eyes. When I looked again the garden was gone, and I knew not where I was, and presently all my dreams were gone. The chips were flying bravely from the stone under my chisel at last, and all my thoughts now were in my carving, when I heard my name, 'Walter,' called, and when I looked down I saw one standing below me, whom I had seen in my dreams just before—Amyot. I had no hopes of seeing him for a long time, perhaps I might never see him again, I thought, for he was away (as I thought) fighting in the holy wars, and it made me almost beside myself to see him standing close by me in the flesh. I got down from my scaffolding as soon as I could, and all thoughts else were soon drowned in the joy of having him by me; Margaret, too, how glad she must have been, for she had been betrothed to him for some time before he want to the wars, and he had been five years away; five years! and how we had thought of him through those many weary days! how often his face had come before me! his brave, honest face, the most beautiful among all the faces of men and women I have ever seen. Yes, I remember how five years ago I held his hand as we came together out of the cathedral of that great, far-off city, whose name I forget now; and then I remember the stamping of the horses' feet; I remember how his hand left mine at last, and then, some one looking back at me earnestly as they all rode on together—looking back, with his hand on the saddle behind him, while the trumpets sang in long solemn peals as they all rode on together, with the glimmer of arms and the fluttering of banners, and the clinking of the rings of the mail, that sounded like the falling of many drops of water into the deep, still waters of some pool that the rocks nearly meet over; and the gleam and flash of the swords, and the glimmer of the lance-heads and the flutter of the rippled banners, that streamed out from them, swept past me, and were gone, and they seemed like a pageant in a dream, whose meaning we know not; and those sounds too, the trumpets, and the clink of the mail, and the thunder of the horse-hoofs, they seemed dream-like too—and it was all like a dream that he should leave me, for we had said that we should always be together; but he went away, and now he is come back again.

We were by his bed-side, Margaret and I; I stood and leaned over him and my hair fell sideways over my face and touched his face; Margaret kneeled beside me, quivering in every limb, not with pain, I think, but rather shaken by a passion of earnest prayer. After some time (I know not how long), I looked up from his face to the window underneath which he lay; I do not know what time of the day it was, but I know that it was a glorious

autumn day, a day soft with melting, golden haze: a vine and a
rose grew together, and trailed half across the window, so that I
could not see much of the beautiful blue sky, and nothing of
town or country beyond; the vine leaves were touched with red
here and there, and three over-blown roses, light pink roses,
hung amongst them. I remember dwelling on the strange lines
the autumn had made in red on one of the gold-green vine
leaves, and watching one leaf of one of the over-blown roses,
expecting it to fall every minute; but as I gazed, and felt disappointed that the rose leaf had not fallen yet, I felt my pain
suddenly shoot through me, and I remembered what I had lost;
and then came bitter, bitter dreams,—dreams which had once
made me happy,—dreams of the things I had hoped would be, of
the things that would never be now; they came between the fair
vine leaves and rose blossoms, and that which lay before the
window; they came as before, perfect in colour and form, sweet
sounds and shapes. But now in every one was something un-
utterably miserable; they would not go away, they put out the
steady glow of the golden haze, the sweet light of the sun
through the vine leaves, the soft leaning of the full blown roses.
I wandered in them for a long time; at last I felt a hand put me
aside gently, for I was standing at the head of—of the bed; then
some one kissed my forehead, and words were spoken—I know
not what words. The bitter dreams left me for the bitterer reality
at last; for I had found him that morning lying dead, only the
morning after I had seen him when he had come back from his
long absence—I had found him lying dead, with his hands
crossed downwards, with his eyes closed, as though the angels
had done that for him; and now when I looked at him he still lay
there, and Margaret knelt by him with her face touching his: she
was not quivering now, her lips moved not at all as they had done
just before; and so, suddenly those words came to my mind
which she had spoken when she kissed me, and which at the
time I had only heard with my outward hearing, for she had said,
'Walter, farewell, and Christ keep you; but for me, I must be with

him, for so I promised him last night that I would never leave
him any more, and God will let me go.' And verily Margaret and
Amyot did go, and left me very lonely and sad.

It was just beneath the westernmost arch of the nave, there I
carved their tomb: I was a long time carving it; I did not think I
should be so long as first, and I said, 'I shall die when I have
finished carving it,' thinking that would be a very short time. But
so it happened after I had carved those two whom I loved, lying
with clasped hands like husband and wife above their tomb, that
I could not yet leave carving it; and so that I might be near them
I became a monk, and used to sit in the choir and sing, thinking
of the time when we should all be together again. And as I had
time I used to go to the westernmost arch of the nave and work
at the tomb that was there under the great, sweeping arch; and in
process of time I raised a marble canopy that reached quite up to
the top of the arch, and I painted it too as fair as I could, and
carved it all about with many flowers and histories, and in them
I carved the faces of those I had known on earth (for I was not as
one on earth now, but seemed quite away out of the world). And
as I carved, sometimes the monks and other people too would
come and gaze, and watch how the flowers grew; and sometimes
too as they gazed, they would weep for pity, knowing how all had
been. So my life passed, and I lived in that abbey for twenty years
after he died, till one morning, quite early, when they came into
the church for matins, they found me lying dead, with my chisel
in my hand, underneath the last lily of the tomb.

MANIFESTO OF THE
SOCIETY FOR THE PROTECTION
OF ANCIENT BUILDINGS

1877

[The first meeting of the SPAB was held on the evening of 22 March 1877 in Morris and Co.'s premises at 26 Queen Square. The ten people in attendance voted Morris honorary secretary and treasurer. A subcommittee consisting of Morris, the firm's business manager George Wardle, and the architect Philip Webb was charged with drawing up a 'statement of principles' for the new Society. The manifesto, ready in draft form by 3 April (Kelvin (ed.), *Collected Letters*, I, p. 359), seems largely to have been Morris's work.—CM]

Society coming before the public with such a name as that above written must needs explain how, and why, it proposes to protect those ancient buildings which, to most people doubtless, seems to have so many and such excellent protectors. This, then, is the explanation we offer.

No doubt within the last fifty years a new interest, almost like another sense, has arisen in these ancient monuments of art; and they have become the subject of one of the most interesting of studies, and of an enthusiasm, religious, historical, artistic, which is one of the undoubted gains of our time; yet we think that if the present treatment of them be continued, our descendants will find them useless for study and chilling to enthusiasm. We think that those last fifty years of knowledge and attention have done more for their destruction than all the foregoing centuries of revolution, violence, and contempt.

For Architecture, long decaying, died out, as a popular art at least, just as the knowledge of medieval art was born. So that the civilised world of the nineteenth century has no style of its own amidst its wide knowledge of the styles of other centuries. From this lack and this gain arose in men's minds the strange idea of the Restoration of ancient buildings; and a strange and most fatal idea, which by its very name implies that it is possible to strip from a building this, that, and the other part of its history—of its life that is—and then to stay the hand at some arbitrary point, and leave it still historical, living, and even as it once was.

In early times this kind of forgery was impossible, because knowledge failed the builders, or perhaps because instinct held them back. If repairs were needed, if ambition or piety pricked on to change, that change was of necessity wrought in the unmistakable fashion of the time; a church of the eleventh century might be added to or altered in the twelfth, thirteenth, fourteenth, fifteenth, sixteenth, or even the seventeenth or eighteenth centuries, but every change, whatever history it destroyed, left history in the gap, and was alive with the spirit of the deeds done midst its fashioning. The result of all this was often a building in which the many changes, though harsh and visible enough, were, by their very contrast, interesting and instructive and could by no possibility mislead. But those who make the changes wrought in our day under the name of Restoration, while professing to bring back a building to the best time of its history, have no guide but each his own individual whim to point out to them what is admirable and what contemptible; while the very nature of their task compels them to destroy something and to supply the gap by imagining what the earlier builders should or might have done. Moreover, in the course of this double process of destruction and addition the whole surface of the building is necessarily tampered with; so that the appearance of antiquity is taken away

from such old parts of the fabric as are left, and there is no laying
to rest in the spectator the suspicion of what may have been lost;
and in short, a feeble and lifeless forgery is the final result of all
the wasted labour.

It is sad to say, that in this manner most of the bigger
Minsters, and a vast number of more humble buildings, both in
England and on the Continent, have been dealt with by men of
talent often, and worthy of better employment, but deaf to the
claims of poetry and history in the highest sense of the words.

For what is left we plead before our architects themselves,
before the official guardians of buildings, and before the public
generally, and we pray them to remember how much is gone of
the religion, thought and manners of time past, never by almost
universal consent, to be Restored; and to consider whether it be
possible to Restore those buildings, the living spirit of which, it
cannot be too often repeated, was an inseparable part of that
religion and thought, and those past manners. For our part we
assure them fearlessly, that of all the Restorations yet undertaken
the worst have meant the reckless stripping [from] a building of
some of its most interesting material features; while the best have
their exact analogy in the Restoration of an old picture, where the
partly-perished work of the ancient craftsmaster has been made
neat and smooth by the tricky hand of some unoriginal and
thoughtless hack of today. If, for the rest, it be asked us to specify
what kind of amount of art, style, or other interest in a building,
makes it worth protecting, we answer, anything which can be
looked on as artistic, picturesque, historical, antique, or subs-
tantial: any work in short, over which educated, artistic people
would think it worthwhile to argue at all.

It is for all these buildings, therefore, of all times and styles,
that we plead, and call upon those who have to deal with them to
put Protection in the place of Restoration, to stave off decay by
daily care, to prop a perilous wall or mend a leaky roof by such
means as are obviously meant for support or covering, and show

no pretence of other art, and otherwise to resist all tampering with either the fabric or ornament of the building as it stands; if it has become inconvenient for its present use, to raise another building rather than alter or enlarge the old one; in fine to treat our ancient buildings as monuments of a bygone art, created by bygone manners, that modern art cannot meddle with without destroying.

Thus, and thus only, shall we escape the reproach of our learning being turned into a snare to us; thus, and thus only can we protect our ancient buildings, and hand them down instructive and venerable to those that come after us.

ADDRESS TO THE FIRST ANNUAL GENERAL MEETING OF THE SOCIETY FOR THE PROTECTION OF ANCIENT BUILDINGS

1878

In putting forth this First Annual Report since the institution of our Society, the Committee cannot but regret, considering how widely-spread and rapid has been both the destruction and falsification of our ancient monuments during the last twenty years, that some such society as this was not long ago called into existence; a society with the principal aim of guarding the life and soul of those monuments, so to speak, and not their bodies merely; a society that might have impressed upon the public the duty of preserving jealously the very gifts that our forefathers left us, and not merely their sites and names.

This lack heretofore of such a body as ours (the result among us, who love art and history, of timidity, or despair) perhaps is, the Committee thinks, all the more to be regretted as its existence for the past year has brought out the fact that there has been lying, little expressed, a great amount of public opinion in favour of the principles which it represents. Some part of this opinion has already attached itself openly to the Society, and more, we doubt not, will every day be attracted to it, and will express itself by its means. But apart from this open and obvious support, we think that the Society will act upon a much greater body of the public, so that its views will grow steadily and insensibly, and become more or less the views held both by the guardians of our ancient buildings, and also by those professional gentlemen in whose hands the fate of these works of art to a great measure lies.

The Committee therefore thinks that the main business of the Society, and surely a very useful one, is this putting forward a rallying point for the collecting and expressing of that rational opinion on this matter, which it once hoped, and now knows for certain, exists abundantly in this country.

As for the means by which the Committee has tried to keep itself before the public; it has taken in hand a great deal of work, which has hitherto necessarily been of a more or less tentative nature, but has certainly sufficed to show how much it may find to do, which may help its purpose of turning public attention to the intrinsic value of our ancient buildings, and the grievous loss we incur by their destruction, and of teaching how much that value, both artistic and historical, depends on their being preserved in a genuine condition. As the sphere and influence of the Society spreads, new channels will doubtless be found in which to direct its energies. One of these, for example, the Committee may be allowed to suggest even now. Up to the present time the Society has confined its efforts to the defence of the monuments of our own country, but, of course, it cannot be unconscious how much such efforts are needed for the preservation of the interest that is yet left to the ancient buildings of the rest of Europe; in many parts of which there has both been more to destroy and more ignorant and reckless destruction than in England. The magnitude of the undertaking only has prevented the Committee from taking active measures in this most important matter, in which, for the rest, it is convinced that there is little time to be lost, if anything is to be done.

To go into details as to the direct work of the Society since its foundation, it has received a great number of letters from various parts of the kingdom relating to demolition and so-called restoration, contemplated or in progress. Every case thus brought under the notice of the Committee has received its careful attention, and where there has seemed to be a possibility of the Society using its influence to any good purpose, steps have been taken to carry out their views. protests have been written and sent to the proper authorities in about forty instances of contemplated restoration or destruction. Members of the Committee have reported after personal visits in many cases, and have used their personal influence to prevent harm being done. It is difficult to tell what direct effect the protests of the Society may have had, but in some cases have come without our notice where the Society's protests have been directly successful, and we are satisfied that in most we have strengthened the hands of those who were opposing the proposed so-called restorations, and have minimized the harm done, and have made it more difficult to tamper with other works of art in the neighbourhood.

It is obviously most important to the Society in carrying out its work, nay, it is a foundation as it were of that work, that it should have correct and detailed information concerning those ancient buildings left more or less untampered with. As one convenient and direct way of obtaining such information, the Committee has had printed a tabular form for giving the complete description of a church, which will shortly be in the hands of every member of the Society; and it hopes to obtain, also, additional help in this matter by sending these out to the clergy far and wide. By this and other means it expects to get a tolerably complete list of all the unrestored churches in Great Britain; and it is to be hoped that every member of the Society will take up the matter as one of personal interest to himself. It may be mentioned here that a member of the Committee, Mr. Coventry Patmore, has suggested (by letter) the publishing of a pamphlet, to be made up from the materials so collected, and has offered to subscribe the sum of £10 towards a special fund for this purpose. As the Committee thoroughly approves of Mr. Patmore's suggestion, and as the ordinary funds of the Society will not allow of devoting money to such publication, it gratefully accepted Mr. Patmore's munificent offer, and is glad now to lay the fact before the Society at large. As to the information already collected on this head, the Committee has information of 749 ancient and quite unrestored churches in England and Wales. Of these the greater number are situated in the counties of Buckinghamshire, Essex, Suffolk, Norfolk, Lincolnshire, and Oxfordshire. They have at present not been able to collect much reliable information respecting the unrestored churches in the counties of Northumberland, Cumberland, Westmorland, Durham, Lancashire, Shropshire, Gloucestershire, Northamptonshire, Herefordshire, Rutland, Huntingdonshire, and Hampshire, or the counties of Wales; nor has their present information dealt much with Scotland nor Ireland. The subject is, however, being attended to by your Committee, and it is hoped that by next autumn a body of information will have been obtained about these localities that may put most of them on the same footing as the counties already dealt with. It is encouraging to remark that so great has been the mass of fine architecture left us by our ancestors, that in spite of all the damage done by restoration and destruction, there is still much left quite untouched, besides what has been left not utterly falsified. The county of Surrey has suffered most—almost, indeed, to the extinction of genuinely ancient buildings; Essex (a county of small and unpretending, though often most interesting, churches) has perhaps suffered least; and Norfolk may be set beside it, a happy fact when we think of its riches in furniture, stained glass, and the like.

The Committee would call attention here to the immense help that the various archaeological and architectural societies throughout the kingdom would be to us in this collecting of information, if they would consent to set their hands to the work—a work, we should think, very congenial to many of their members.

The Committee has devoted much attention to the dissemination of pamphlets bearing directly upon the evils of restoration, thinking that by this means the aims and scope of the Society will become more generally understood and appreciated. Many of its members have been most active in expressing its views publicly, and these utterances your Committee has made it part of its business to circulate. Of these we may mention Mr. J.J. Stevenson's paper, read before the Institute of Architects last year, and which excited much attention at the time. Last March Mr. G. Aitcheson read a paper on the subject before the Social Science Congress at Aberdeen, and last September another paper before the Art Club at Liverpool. The Rev. W.J. Loftie contributed an article to *MacMillan's Magazine* in June of last year, which brought out much discussion, and Professor Colvin last October did as much in the *Nineteenth Century*. All these papers have been widely circulated, together with the now famous and most eloquent passage from Professor John Ruskin's "Seven Lamps of Architecture"; a protest unfortunately as much needed now as it was years ago. As a matter of course, also, the paper first put forth by the Society has been sent on every occasion of calling attention to the Society's existence.

The Committee is happy to call the attention of the Society to some causes for congratulation. It has had encouraging correspondence in many cases, both with the clergy and patrons of livings, who have asked for advice in dealing with the necessary repairs of the buildings under their care. The Society has already been much noticed by the Press, always with respect, and generally with unqualified approval. The *Athenaeum*, which has the honourable distinction of having for years past steadily and courageously resisted the follies of Restoration, has never failed in its support of the Society; *Punch* has given us good help both with pen and pencil; and a clever artist in *Fun* has seen his opportunity in the subject, and seized upon it with goodwill. There have been serious and for the most part sympathetic articles on the Society in the *Globe, Daily Telegraph, Daily News, Guardian, Architect, Whitehall Review, Graphic, Truth*, &c., besides many of the leading country journals; and we have every reason to believe that these articles reflect a growing feeling in favour of our principles, both among men and women, throughout the country.

Nevertheless, the work to be done is heavy; and even now mere cynically brutal destruction, not veiling itself under any artistic pretence, is only too common: It is still only too commonly assumed that any considerations of Art must yield if they stand in the way of money interests. In fact, it is hard to convince people in general that the art in our ancient buildings is a real solid possession. The Committee thinks it timely to call your attention here to the threatened gradual destruction of what is left of the old churches in the City of London. We have only to think of London deprived of the interest and variety that their steeples give to it, to get an idea of how grievous their loss will be. Historic, curious, characteristic, and in many cases beautiful, there must be few people indeed of any cultivation who will not regret them. Scarcely anyone, we think, of [sic] any feeling for art, history, or civilization, who will not echo the following words of one of our greatest authors, which the Committee is happy to insert in this Report:

Mr. Thomas Carlyle writes to us thus on the subject: "I can have but little hope that any word of mine can help you in your good work of trying to save the Wren Churches in the City from destruction; but my clear feeling is, that it would be a sordid, nay sinful, piece of barbarism to do other than religiously preserve these churches as precious heirlooms; many of them specimens of noble architecture, the like of which we have no prospect of ever being able to produce in England again."

We do find it strange, indeed, that the richest country and city in the world grudges to the Arts the few feet of ground that these ancient monuments occupy; and the Committee thinks it a worthy work of this Society to rouse public opinion on the subject, and call the attention of the public to the loss that they are sustaining in the demolition of these buildings, which are nearly all doomed, and are coming down quietly but surely, church after church; it is the intention, therefore, of the Committee to publish a pamphlet, and to take other measures with this object, shortly.

Before making an end of this report, the Committee would like to call the attention both of members of the Society and of the public generally to two points especially on which the Society is likely to be misunderstood. We have probably all of us heard our Society accused, in the face of the declaration of the first paper we put forth, of being ourselves the favourers of that ruin and destruction from which we profess to defend our ancient monuments. We should like to protest once more against this misunderstanding, and to declare what a grief it is to us to come across the results, the unfortunately irreparable results, of neglect and brutality, and what a pleasure to look on a building which, owing to reverent and constant care, still stands trim and sound, with no wilfulness of which to accuse the hand of man, with nothing to regret except the inevitable lapse of time, and the slow and gentle decay it has brought with it; and how slow that may be, the most ancient buildings in the world yet bear witness, and will do so for many a hundred years.

Again, to look facts in the face once more, we have many of us met with a tendency to saddle on us an undue regard for certain forms of art, certain styles of architecture; an accusation (as we must call it) founded on the necessity our principles enforce upon us to protest against the wholesale contempt, and consequent widespread destruction, of all the architectural works accomplished in this country after a certain date. We desire to declare emphatically that the Society neither has the will nor the power to enter into any "battle of the styles;" and we beg to inform the public that it counts amongst its members persons of every shade of artistic opinion, and differing widely in their artistic sympathies, whose common bond is earnest opposition at once to neglect and meddling in matters concerning all buildings that have any claim to be considered works of art. Our enemies are the enemies of the works of all styles alike, ignorant destruction and pedantic reconstruction.

To conclude: if only we can get a little breathing-space we believe that this Society will be of at least some service; we think that there are many among those who have to deal with ancient buildings, who do really feel the force of our reasoning on this matter, and that already restorations when they take place stand a good chance of not being so sweeping as they once would have been. Many other persons of cultivation also we believe do really at heart fully agree with us, and probably no few of these would openly join the Society if they did not belong to that class of mind which the enunciation of any principle frightens. These last, men rather too logical to be thoroughly practical, we would remind of the necessity of having some distinct rallying-point for collecting the genuine feeling on this subject, hitherto scattered and helpless; and then, that necessity being admitted, we would further remind them of the need of some wide but distinctly enounced test, to serve as a bond for that unity of thought and action, which alone can impress the public with the sense of a growing feeling, founded upon reason and common sense.

THE PROSPECTS OF ARCHITECTURE IN CIVILISATION

1881

'—the horrible doctrine that this universe is a Cockney Nightmare—
which no creature ought for a moment to believe or listen to.'
—THOMAS CARLYLE.

The word Architecture has, I suppose, to most of you the meaning of the art of building nobly and ornamentally. Now, I believe the practice of this art to be one of the most important things which man can turn his hand to, and the consideration of it to be worth the attention of serious people, not for an hour only, but for a good part of their lives, even though they may not have to do with it professionally.

But, noble as that art is by itself, and though it is specially the art of civilisation, it neither ever has existed nor ever can exist alive and progressive by itself, but must cherish and be cherished by all the crafts whereby men make the things which they intend shall be beautiful, and shall last somewhat beyond the passing day.

It is this union of the arts, mutually helpful and harmoniously subordinated one to another, which I have learned to think of as Architecture, and when I use the word to-night, that is what I shall mean by it and nothing narrower.

A great subject truly, for it embraces the consideration of the whole external surroundings of the life of man; we cannot escape from it if we would so long as we are part of civilisation, for it means the moulding and altering to human needs of the very face of the earth itself, except in the outermost desert.

Neither can we hand over our interests in it to a little band of learned men, and bid them seek and discover, and fashion, that we may at last stand by and wonder at the work, and learn a little of how 'twas all done: 'tis we ourselves, each one of us, who must keep watch and ward over the fairness of the earth, and each with his own soul and hand do his due share therein, lest we deliver to our sons a lesser treasurer than our fathers left to us.

Nor, again, is there time enough and to spare that we may leave this matter alone till our latter days or let our sons deal with it: for so busy and eager is mankind, that the desire of to-day makes us utterly forget the desire of yesterday and the gain it brought; and whensoever in any object of pursuit we cease to long for perfection, corruption sure and speedy leads from life to death and all is soon over and forgotten: time enough there may be for many things: for peopling the desert; for breaking down the walls between nation and nation; for learning the innermost secrets of the fashion of our souls and bodies, the air we breathe, and the earth we tread on: time enough for subduing all the forces of nature to our material wants: but no time to spare before we turn our eyes and our longing to the fairness of the earth; lest the wave of human need sweep over it and make it not a hopeful desert as it once was, but a hopeless prison: lest man should find at last that he has toiled and striven, and conquered, and set all things on the earth under his feet, that he might live thereon himself unhappy.

Most true it is that when any spot on earth's surface has been marred by the haste or carelessness of civilisation, it is heavy work to seek a remedy, nay a work scarce conceivable; for the desire to live on any terms which nature has implanted in us, and the terribly swift multiplication of the race which is the result of it, thrusts out of men's minds all thought of other hopes and bars the way before us as with a wall of iron: no force but a force equal to that which marred can ever mend, or give back those ruined places to hope and civilisation.

Therefore I entreat you to turn your minds to thinking of what is to come of Architecture, that is to say, the fairness of the earth amidst the habitations of men: for the hope and the fear of it will follow us though we try to escape it; it concerns us all, and needs the help of all; and what we do herein must be done at once, since every day of our neglect adds to the heap of troubles a blind force is making for us; till it may come to this if we do not look to it, that we shall one day have to call, not on peace and prosperity, but on violence and ruin to rid us of them.

In making this appeal to you, I will not suppose that I am speaking to any who refuse to admit that we who are part of civilisation are responsible to posterity for what may befall the fairness of the earth in our own days, for what we have done, in other words, towards the progress of Architecture; if any such exist among cultivated people, I need not trouble myself about them; for they would not listen to me, nor should I know what to say to them.

On the other hand, there may be some here who have a knowledge of their responsibility in this matter, but to whom the duty that it involves seems an easy one, since they are fairly satisfied with the state of architecture as it now is: I do not suppose that they fail to note the strange contrast which exists between the beauty that still clings to some habitations of men, and the ugliness which is the rule in others, but it seems to them natural and inevitable, and therefore does not trouble them: and they fulfill their duties to civilisation and the arts by sometimes going to see the beautiful places, and gathering together a few matters to remind them of these for the adornment of the ugly dwellings in which their homes are enshrined: for the rest they have no doubt that it is natural and not wrong that while all ancient towns, I mean towns whose houses are largely ancient, should be beautiful and romantic, all modern ones should be ugly and commonplace: it does not seem to them that this contrast is of any import to civilisation, or that it expresses anything save that one town *is* ancient as to its buildings and the other modern. If their thoughts carry them into looking any farther into the contrast between ancient art and modern, they are not dissatisfied with the result: they may see things to reform here and there, but they suppose, or, let me say, take for granted, that art is alive and healthy, is on the right road, and that following that road, it will go on living for ever, much as it is now.

It is not unfair to say that this languid complacency is the general attitude of cultivated people towards the arts: of course if they were ever to think seriously of them, they would be startled into discomfort by the thought that civilisation as it now is brings inevitable ugliness with it: surely if they thought this, they would begin to think that this was not natural and right; they would see that this was not what civilisation aimed at in its struggling days: but they do not think seriously of the arts because they have been hitherto defended by a law of nature which forbids men to see evils which they are not ready to redress.

Hitherto: but there are not wanting signs that that defence may fail them one day, and it has become the duty of all true artists, and all men who love life though it be troublous better than death though it be peaceful, to strive to pierce that defence and to string the world, cultivated and uncultivated, into discontent and struggle.

Therefore I will say that the contrast between past art and present, the universal beauty of men's habitations as they *were* fashioned, and the universal ugliness of them as they *are* fashioned, is of the utmost import to civilisation, and that it expresses much, it expresses no less than a blind brutality which will destroy art at least, whatever else it may leave alive: art is not healthy, it even scarcely lives; it is on the wrong road, and if it follow that road will speedily meet its death on it.

Now perhaps you will say that by asserting that the general attitude of cultivated people towards the arts is a languid complacency with this unhealthy state of things, I am admitting that cultivated people generally do not care about the arts, and that therefore this threatened death of them will not frighten people much, even if the threat be founded on truth: so that those are but beating the air who strive to rouse people into discontent and struggle.

Well, I will run the risk of offending you by speaking plainly, and saying, that to me it seems over true that cultivated people in general do *not* care about the arts: nevertheless I will answer any possible challenge as to the usefulness of trying to rouse them to thought about the matter, by saying that they do not care about the arts because they do not know what they mean, or what they lose in lacking them: cultivated, that is rich, as they are, they also are under that harrow of hard necessity which is driven onward so remorselessly by the competitive commerce of the latter days; a system which is drawing near now I hope to its perfection, and therefore to its death and change: the many millions of civilisation, as labour is now organised, can scarce think seriously of anything but the means of earning their daily bread; they do not know of art, it does not touch their lives at all: the few thousands of cultivated people, whom fate, not always as kind to them as she looks, has placed above the material necessity for this hard struggle, are nevertheless bound by it in spirit: the reflex of the grinding trouble of those who toil to live that they may live to toil weighs upon them also, and forbids them to look upon art as a matter of importance: they know it but as a toy, not as a serious help to life: as they know it, it can no more lift the burden from the conscience of the rich, than it can from the weariness of the poor. They do not know what art means: as I have said, they think as labour is now organised art can go indefinitely as *it* is now organised, practised by a few for a few, adding a little interest, a little refinement to the lives of those who have come to look upon intellectual interest, and spiritual refinement as their birthright.

No, no, it can never be: believe me if it were otherwise possible that it should be an enduring condition of humanity that there must be one class utterly refined and another utterly brutal, art would bar the way and forbid the monstrosity to exist: such refinement would have to do as well as it might without the aid of art: it may be she will die, but it cannot be that she will live the slave of the rich, and the token of the enduring slavery of the poor. If the life of the world is to be brutalised by her death, the rich must share that brutalization with the poor.

I know that there are people of good-will now, as there have been in all ages, who have conceived of art as going hand in hand with luxury, nay, as being much the same thing; but it is an idea false from the root up, and most hurtful to art, as I could demonstrate to you by many examples if I had time, lacking which I will only meet it with one, which I hope will be enough.

We are here in the richest city of the richest country of the richest age of the world: no luxury of time past can compare with our luxury; and yet if you could clear your eyes from habitual blindness you would have to confess that there is no crime against art, no ugliness, no vulgarity which is not shared with perfect fairness and equality between the modern hovels of Bethnal Green and the modern palaces of the West End: and then if you looked at the matter deeply and seriously you would not regret it, but rejoice at it, and as you went past some notable example of the aforesaid palaces you would exult indeed as you say, 'So that is all that luxury and money can do for refinement.'

For the rest, if of late there has been any change for the better in the prospects of the arts; if there has been a struggle both to throw off the chains of dead and powerless tradition, and to understand the thoughts and aspirations of those among whom those traditions were once alive powerful and beneficent; if there has been abroad any spirit of resistance to the flood of sordid ugliness that modern civilisation has created to make modern civilisation miserable: in a word, if any of us have had the courage to be discontented that art seems dying, and to hope for her new birth, it is because others have been discontented and hopeful in other matters than the arts: I believe most sincerely that the steady progress of those whom the stupidity of language forces me to call the lower classes in material, political and social condition, has been our real help in all that we have been able to do or to hope, although both the helpers and the helped have been mostly unconscious of it.

It is indeed in this belief, the belief in the beneficent progress of civilisation, that I venture to face you and to entreat you to strive to enter into the real meaning of the arts, which are surely the expression of reverence for nature, and the crown of the nature, the life of man upon the earth.

With this intend in view I may, I think, hope to move you, I do not say to agree to all I urge upon you, yet at least to think the matter worth thinking about; and if you once do that, I believe I shall have won you. Maybe indeed that many things which I think beautiful you will deem of small account; nay that even some things I think base and ugly will not vex your eyes or your minds: but one thing I know you will none of you like to plead guilty to; blindness to the natural beauty of the earth; and of that beauty art is the only possible guardian.

No one of you can fail to know what neglect of art has done to this great treasure of mankind: the earth which was beautiful before man lived on it, which for many ages grew in beauty as men grew in numbers and power, is now growing uglier day by day, and there the swiftest where civilisation is the mightiest: this is quite certain; no one can deny it: are you contented that it should be so?

Surely there must be few of us to whom this degrading change has not been brought home personally. I think you will most of you understand me but too well when I ask you to remember the pang of dismay that comes on us when we revisit some spot of country which has been specially sympathetic to us in times past; which has refreshed us after toil, or soothed us after trouble; but where now as we turn the corner of the road or crown the hill's brow we can see first the inevitable blue slate roof, and then the blotched mud-coloured stucco, or ill-built wall of ill-made bricks of the new buildings; than as we come nearer, and see the arid and pretentious little gardens, and cast-iron horrors of railings, and miseries of squalid outhouses breaking through the sweet meadows and abundant hedge-rows of our old quiet hamlet, do not our hearts sink within us, and are we not troubled with a perplexity not altogether selfish, when we think what a little bit of carelessness it takes to destroy a world of pleasure and delight, which now whatever happens can never be recovered?

Well may we feel the perplexity and sickness of heart, which some day the whole world shall feel to find its hopes disappointed, if we do not look to it; for this is not what civilisation looked for: a new house added to the old village, where is the harm of that? Should it not have been a gain and not a loss; a sign of growth and prosperity which should have rejoiced the eye of an old friend? a new family come in health and hope to share the modest pleasures and labours of the place we loved; that should have been no grief, but a fresh pleasure to us.

Yes, and time was that it would have been so: the new house indeed would have taken away a little piece of the flowery green sward, a few yards of the teeming hedge-row; but a new order, a new beauty would have taken the place of the old: the very flowers of the field would have but given place to flowers fashioned by man's hand and mind: the hedge-row oak would have blossomed into fresh beauty in roof-tree and lintel and door-post: and though the new house would have looked young and trim beside the older houses and the ancient church; ancient even in those days; yet it would have a piece of history for the time to come, and its dear and dainty cream-white walls would have been a genuine link among the numberless links of that long chain, whose beginnings we know not of but on whose mighty length even the many-pillared garth of Pallas, and the stately dome of the Eternal Wisdom, are but single links, wondrous and resplendent though they be.

Such I say can a new house be, such it has been: for 'tis no ideal house I am thinking of: no rare marvel of art, of which but few can ever be vouchsafed to the best times and countries: no palace either, not even a manor-house, but a yeoman's steading at grandest, or even his shepherd's cottage: there they stand at this day, dozens of them yet, in some parts of England: such an one, and of the smallest, is before my eyes as I speak to you, standing by the roadside on one of the western slopes of the Cotswolds: the tops of the great trees near it can see a long way off the mountains of the Welsh border, and between a great county of hill, and waving woodland, and meadow and plain where lies hidden many a famous battle-field of our stout forefathers: there to the right a wavering patch of blue is the smoke of Worcester town, but Evesham smoke though near, is unseen, so small it is: then a long line of haze just traceable shows where Avon wends its way thence towards. Severn, till Bredon Hill hides the sight both of it and Tewkesbury smoke: just below on either side the Broadway lie the grey houses of the village street ending with a lovely house of the fourteenth century; above the road winds serpentine up the steep hill-side, whose crest looking westward sees the glorious map I have been telling of spread before it, but eastward strains to look on Oxfordshire, and thence all waters run towards Thames: all about lie the sunny slopes, lovely of outline, flowery and sweetly grassed, dotted with the best-grown and most graceful of trees: 'tis a beautiful country side indeed, not undignified, not unromantic, but most familiar.

And there stands the little house that was new once, a labourer's cottage built of the Cotswold limestone, and grown now, walls and roof, a lovely warm grey, though it was creamy white in its earliest day; no line of it could ever have marred the Cotswold beauty; everything about it is solid and well wrought: it is skilfully planned and well proportioned: there is a little sharp and delicate carving about its arched doorway, and every part of it is well cared for: 'tis in fact beautiful, a work of art and a piece of nature—no less: there is no man who could have done it better considering its use and its place.

Who built it then? No strange race of men, but just the mason of Broadway village: even such a man as is now running up down yonder three or four cottages of the wretched type we know too well: nor did he get an architect from London, or even Worcester, to design it: I believe 'tis but two hundred years old, and at that time, though beauty still lingered among the peasants' houses, your learned architects were building houses for the high gentry that were ugly enough, though solid and well built; not are its materials far-fetched; from the neighbouring field came its walling stones; and at the top of the hill they are quarrying now as good freestone as ever.

No, there was no effort or wonder about it when it was built, though its beauty makes it strange now.

And are you contented that we should lose all this; this simple harmless beauty that was no hindrance or trouble to any man, and that added to the natural beauty of the earth instead of marring it?

You cannot be contented with it; all you can do is to try to forget it, and to say that such things are the necessary and inevitable consequences of civilisation. Is it so indeed? The loss of such-like beauty is an undoubted evil: but civilisation cannot mean at heart to produce evils for mankind: such losses therefore must be accidents of civilisation, produced by its carelessness, not its malice: and we, if we be men and not machines, must try to amend them: or civilisation itself will be undone.

But now let us leave the sunny slopes of the Cotswolds, and

their little grey houses, lest we fall a-dreaming over past time, and let us think about the suburbs of London, neither dull nor unpleasant once, where surely we ought to have some power to do something: let me remind you how it fares with the beauty of the earth when some big house near our dwelling-place, which has passed through many vicissitudes of rich merchant's dwelling, school, hospital, or what not, is at last to be turned into ready money, and is sold to A, who lets it to B, who is going to build houses on it which he will sell to C, who will let them to D and the other letters of the alphabet: well, the old house comes down; that was to be looked for, and perhaps you don't much mind it; it was never a work of art, was stupid and unimaginative enough, though creditably built, and without pretence; but even while it is being pulled down, you hear the axe falling on the trees of its generous garden, which it was such a pleasure even to pass by, and where man and nature together have worked so long and patiently for the blessing of the neighbours: so you see the boys dragging about the streets great boughs of the flowering may trees covered with blossom, and you know what is going to happen. Next morning when you get up you look towards that great plane-tree which has been such a friend to you so long through sun and rain and wind, which was a world in itself of incident and beauty: but now there is a gap and no plane-tree; next morning 'tis the turn of the great sweeping layers of darkness that the ancient cedars thrust out from them, very treasures of loveliness and romance; they are gone too: you may have a faint hope left that the thick bank of lilac next to your house may be spared, since the newcomers may like lilac; but 'tis gone in the afternoon, and the next day when you look in with a sore heart, you see that once fair great garden turned into a petty miserable clay-trampled yard, and everything is ready for the latest development of Victorian architecture—which in due time (two months) arises from the wreck.

Do you like it? You, I mean, who have not studied art and do not think you care about it?

Look at the houses (there are plenty to choose from)! I will not say, are they beautiful, for you say you don't care whether they are or not: but just look at the wretched pennyworths of material, of accommodation, of ornament doled out to you! if there were one touch of generosity, of honest pride, of wish to please about them, I would forgive them in the lump. But there is none—not one.

It is for this that you have sacrificed your cedars and plane and may-trees, which I do believe you really liked—are you satisfied?

Indeed you cannot be: all you can do is to go to your business, converse with your family, eat, drink, and sleep, and try to forget it, but whenever you think of it, you will admit that a loss without compensation has befallen you and your neighbours.

Once more neglect of art has done it; for though it is conceivable that the loss of your neighbouring open space might in any case have been a loss to you, still the building of a new quarter of a town ought not to be an unmixed calamity to the neighbours: nor would it have been once: for first, the builder doesn't now murder the trees (at any rate not all of them) for the trifling sum of money their corpses will bring him, but because it will take him too much trouble to fit them into the planning of his houses: so to begin with you would have saved the more part of your trees; and I say *your* trees advisedly, for they were at least as much *your* trees, who loved them and would have saved them as they were the trees of the man who neglected and murdered them. And next, for any space you would have lost, and for any unavoidable destruction of natural growth, you would in the times of art have been compensated by orderly beauty, by visible signs of the ingenuity of man and his delight both in the works of nature and the works of his own hands.

Yes indeed, if we had lived in Venice in early days, as islet after islet was built upon, we should have grudged it but little, I think, though we had been merchants and rich men, that the Greek shafted work, and the carving of the Lombards was drawn nearer and nearer to us and blocked us out a little from the sight of the blue Euganean hills or the Northern mountains. Nay, to come nearer home, much as I know I should have loved the willowy meadows between the network of the streams of Thames and Cherwell; yet I should not have been ill-content as Oxford crept northward from its early home of Oseney, and Rewley, and the Castle, as townsman's house, and scholar's hall, and the great College and the noble church hid year by year more and more of the grass and flowers of Oxfordshire.*

That was the natural course of things then; men could do no otherwise when they built than give some gift of beauty to the world: but all is turned inside out now, and when men build they cannot but take away some gift of beauty, which nature or their own forefathers have given to the world.

Wonderful it is indeed, and perplexing, that the course of civilisation towards perfection should have brought this about: so perplexing, that to some it seems as if civilisation were eating her own children, and the arts first of all.

I will not say that; time is big with so many a change: surely there must be some remedy, and whether there be or no, at least it is better to die seeking one, than to leave it alone and do nothing.

I have said, are you satisfied? and assumed that you are not, though to many you may seem to be at least helpless: yet indeed it is something or even a great deal that I can reasonably assume that you are discontented: fifty years ago, thirty years ago, nay perhaps twenty years ago, it would have been useless to have asked such a question, it could only have been answered in one way: we are perfectly satisfied: where now we may at least hope that discontent will grow till some remedy will be sought for.

---

* Indeed it is a new world now, when the new Cowley dog-holes must needs slay Magdalen Bridge!—*Nov.* 1881.[2]

And if sought for, should it not, in England at least, be as good as found already, and acted upon? At first sight it seems so truly; for I may say without fear of contradiction that we of the English middle-classes are the most powerful body of men that the world has yet seen, and that anything we have set our heart upon we will have: and yet when we come to look the matter in the face, we cannot fail to see that even for us with all our strength it will be a hard matter to bring about that birth of the new art: for between us and that which is to be, if art if not to perish utterly, there is something alive and devouring; something as it were a river of fire that will put all that tries to swim across to a hard proof indeed, and scare from the plunge every soul that is not made fearless by desire of truth and insight of the happy days to come beyond.

That fire is the hurry of life bred by the gradual perfection of competitive commerce which we, the English middle-classes, when we had won our political liberty, set ourselves to further with an energy, an eagerness, a single-heartedness that has no parallel in history; we would suffer none to bar the way to us, we called on none to help us, we thought of that one thing and forgot all else, and so attained to our desire, and fashioned a terrible thing indeed from the very hearts of the strongest of mankind.

Indeed I don't suppose that the feeble discontent with our own creation that I have noted before can deal with such a force as this—not yet—not till it swells to very strong discontent: nevertheless as we were blind to its destructive power, and have not even yet learned all about *that*, so we may well be blind to what it has of constructive force in it, and that one day may give us a chance to deal with it again and turn it toward accomplishing our new and worthier desire: in that day at least when we have at last learned what we want, let us work no less strenuously and fearlessly, I will not say to quench it, but to force it to burn itself out, as we once did to quicken, and sustain it.

Meantime if we could but get ourselves ready by casting off certain old prejudices and delusions in this matter of the arts, we should the sooner reach the pitch of discontent which would drive us into action: such a one I mean as the aforesaid idea that luxury fosters art, and especially the Architectural arts; or its compassion one, that the arts flourish best in a rich country, *i.e.* a country where the contrast between rich and poor is greatest: or this, the worst because the most plausible, the assertion of the hierarchy of intellect in the arts: an old foe with a new face indeed; born out of the times that gave the death-blow to the political and social hierarchies, and waxing as they waned, it proclaimed from a new side the divinity of the few and the subjugation of the many, and cries out, like they did, that it is expedient, not that man should die for the people, but that the people should die for one man.

Now perhaps these three things, though they have different forms, are in fact but one thing; tyranny to wit: but however that may be, they are to be met by one answer, and there is no other: if art which is now sick is to live and not die, it must in the future be of the people, for the people, and by the people; it must understand all and be understood by all: equality must be the answer to tyranny: if that be not attained art will die.

The past art of what has grown to be civilised Europe from the time of the decline of the ancient classical peoples, was the outcome of instinct working on an unbroken chain of tradition: it was fed not by knowledge buy by hope, and though many a strange and wild illusion mingled with that hope, yet was it human and fruitful ever: many a man it solaced, many a slave in body it freed in soul: boundless pleasure it gave to those who wrought it and those who used it: long and long it lived, passing that torch of hope from hand to hand, while it kept but little record of its best and noblest; for least of all things could it abide to make for itself kings and tyrants: every man's hand and soul it used, the lowest as the highest, and in its bosom at least were all men free: it did its work, not creating an art more perfect than itself, but rather other things than art, freedom of thought and speech, and the longing for light and knowledge and the coming days that should slay it: and so as last it died in the hour of its highest hope, almost before the greatest men that came of it has passed away from the world. It is dead now; no longing will bring it back to us; no echo of it is left among the peoples whom it once made happy.

Of the art that is to come who may prophesy? But this at least seems to follow from comparing that past with the confusion in which we are now struggling and the light that glimmers through it: that that art will no longer be an art of instinct, of ignorance which is hopeful to learn and strives to see; since ignorance is now no longer hopeful. In this and in many other ways it may differ from the past art, but in one thing it must needs be like it; it will not be an esoteric mystery shared by a little band of superior beings; it will be no more hierarchical than the art of past time was, but like it will be a gift of the people to the people, a thing which everybody can understand, and everyone surround with love, it will be a part of every life, and a hindrance to none.

For this is the essence of art, and the thing that is eternal to it, whatever else may be passing and accidental.

Here it is, you see, wherein the art of to-day is so far astray, would that I could say wherein it *has been* astray, it has been sick because of this packing and peeling with tyranny, and now with what of life it has it must struggle back towards equality.

There is the hard business for us! to get all simple people to care about art, to get them to insist on making it part of their lives, whatever becomes of systems of commerce and labour held perfect by some of us.

This is henceforward for a long time to come the real business of art: and—yes I will say it since I think it, of civilisation too for that matter: but how shall we set to work about it? How shall we give people without tradition of art eyes with which to see the works we do to move them? How shall we give them leisure from toil and truce with anxiety, so that they may have time to brood over the longing for beauty which men are born with, as 'tis said, even in London streets? And chiefly, for this will breed the others swiftly and certainly, how shall we give them hope and pleasure in their daily work?

How shall we give them this soul of art without which men are worse than savages? If they would but drive us to it! But what and where are the forces that shall drive them to drive us? Where is the lever and the standpoint?

Hard questions indeed! but unless we are prepared to seek an answer for them, our art is a mere toy, which may amuse us for a little, but which will not sustain us at our need: the cultivated classes, as they are called, will feel it slipping away from under them; till some of them will but mock it as a worthless thing; and some will stand by and look at it as a curious exercise of the intellect, useless when done, though amusing to watch a doing. How long will art live on those terms? Yet such were even now the state of art were it not for that hope which I am here to set forth to you, the hope of an art that shall express the soul of the people.

Therefore, I say, that in these days we men of civilisation have to choose if we will cast art aside or not; if we choose to do so I have no more to say, save that we *may* find something to take its place for the solace and joy of mankind, but I scarce think we shall: But if we refuse to cast art aside then must we seek an answer for those hard questions aforesaid, of which is the first?

How shall we set about giving people without traditions of art eyes with which to see works of art? It will doubtless take many years of striving and success, before we can think of answering that question fully: and if we strive to do our duty herein, long before it is answered fully there will be some kind of a popular art abiding among us: but meantime, and setting aside the answer which every artist must make to his own share of the question, there is one duty obvious to us all; it is that we should set ourselves, each one of us, to doing our best to guard the natural beauty of the earth: we ought to look upon it as a crime, an injury to our fellows, only excusable because of ignorance, to mar that natural beauty, which is the property of all men; and scarce less than a crime to look on and do nothing while others are marring it, if we can no longer plead this ignorance.

Now this duty as it is the most obvious to us, and the first and readiest way of giving people back their eyes, so happily it is the easiest to set about; up to a certain point you will have all people of good will to the public good on your side: nay, small as the beginning is, something has actually been begun in this direction, and we may well say considering how hopeless things looked twenty years ago that it is marvellous in our eyes? Yet if we every get out of the troubles that we are now wallowing in, it will seem perhaps more marvellous still to those that come after us that the dwellers in the richest city in the world were at one time rather proud that the members of a small, humble, and rather obscure, though I will say it, a beneficent society, should have felt it their duty to shut their eyes to the apparent hopelessness of attacking with their feeble means the stupendous evils they had become alive to, so that the might be able to make some small beginnings towards awakening the general public to a due sense of those evils.

I say, that though I ask your earnest support for such associations as the Kyrle and the Commons Preservation Societies,[1] and though I feel sure that they have begun at the right end, since neither gods nor governments will help those who don't themselves; though we are bound to wait for nobody's help than our own in dealing with the devouring hideousness and squalor of our great towns, and especially of London, for which the whole country is responsible; yet it would be idle not to acknowledge that the difficulties in our way are far too huge and wide-spreading to be grappled by private or semi-private efforts only.

All we can do in this way we must look on not as palliatives of an unendurable state of things but as tokens of what we desire; which is in short the giving back to our country of the natural beauty of the earth, which we are so ashamed of having taken away from it: and our chief duty herein will be to quicken this shame and the pain that comes from it in the hearts of our fellows: this I say is one of the chief duties of all those who have any right to the title of cultivated men: and I believe that if we are faithful to it, we may help to further a great impulse towards beauty among us, which will be so irresistible that it will fashion for itself a national machinery which will sweep away all difficulties between us and a decent life, though they may have increased a thousand-fold meantime, as is only too like to be the case.

Surely that light will arise, though neither we nor our children's children see it, though civilisation may have to go down into dark places enough meantime: surely one day making will be thought more honourable, more worthy the majesty of a great nation than destruction.

It is strange indeed, it is woeful, it is scarcely comprehensible, if we come to think of it as men, and not as machines, that, after all the progress of civilisation, it should be so easy for a little official talk, a few lines on a sheet of paper to set a terrible engine to work, which without any trouble on our part will slay us ten thousand men, and ruin who can say how many thousand of families; and it lies light enough on the conscience of *all* of us; while if it is a question of striking a blow at grievous and crushing evils which lie at our own doors, evils which every thoughtful man feels and laments, and for which we alone are responsible, not only is there no national machinery for dealing with them, though they grow ranker and ranker every year, but any hint that such a thing may be possible is received with laughter or with terror, or with severe and heavy blame. The rights of property, the necessities of morality, the interests of religion—those are the sacramental words of cowardice that silence us!

Sirs, I have spoken of thoughtful men who feel these evils: but think of all the millions of men whom our civilisation has bred, who are not thoughtful, and have had no chance of being so; how can you fail to acknowledge the duty of defending the fairness of the Earth? and what is the use of our cultivation if it is to cultivate us into cowards? Let us answer those feeble counsels of despair and say, we also have a property which your tyranny of squalor cheats us of: we also have a morality which its baseness crushes; we also have a religion which its injustice makes a mock of.

Well, whatever lesser helps there may be to our endeavour of giving people back the eyes we have robbed them of, we may pass them by at present, for they are chiefly of use to people who are beginning to get their eyesight again; to people who though they have no traditions of art, can study those mighty impulses that once led nations and races: it is to such that museums and art education are of service; but it is clear they cannot get at the great mass of people, who will at present stare at them in unintelligent wonder.

Until our streets are decent and orderly, and our town gardens break the bricks and mortar every here and there, and are open to all people; until our meadows even near our towns become fair and sweet, and are unspoiled by patches of hideousness: until we have clear sky above our heads and green grass beneath our feet; until the great drama of the seasons can touch our workmen with other feelings than the misery of winter and the weariness of summer; till all this happens our museums and art schools will be but amusements of the rich; and they will soon cease to be of any use to them also, unless they make up their minds that they will do their best to give us back the fairness of the Earth.

In what I have been saying on this last point I have been thinking of our own special duties as cultivated people, but in

our endeavours towards this end, as in all others, cultivated
people cannot stand alone; nor can we do much to open people's
eyes till they cry out to us to have them opened. Now I cannot
doubt that the longing to attack and overcome the sordidness of
the city life of to-day still dwells in the minds of workmen, as
well as in ours, but it can scarcely be otherwise than vague and
lacking guidance with men who have so little leisure, and are so
hemmed in with hideousness as they are. So this brings us to our
second question: How shall people in general get leisure enough
from toil and truce enough with anxiety to give scope to their
inborn longing for beauty?

Now the part of this question that is not involved in the next
one, How shall they get proper work to do? is I think in a fair
way to be answered.

The mighty change which the success of competitive commerce has wrought in the world, whatever it may have destroyed,
has at least unwittingly made on thing,—from out of it has been
born the increasing power of the working-class. The determination which this power has bred in it to raise their class as a class
will I doubt not make way and prosper with our goodwill or even
in spite of it: but it seems to me that both to the working class
and especially to ourselves it is important that it should have our
abundant goodwill, and also what help we may be able otherwise
to give it, by our determination to deal fairly with workmen,
even when that justice may seem to involve our own loss. The
time of unreasonable and blind outcry against the Trades Unions
is, I am happy to think, gone by; and has given place to the hope
of a time when these great Associations, well organized, well
served, and earnestly supported, as I *know* them to be, will find
other work before them than the temporary support of their
members and the adjustment of due wages for their crafts: when
that hope begins to be realised, and they find they can make use
of the help of us scattered units of the cultivated classes, I feel

sure that the claims of art, as we and they will then understand the word, will by no means be disregarded by them.

Meantime with us who are called artists, since most un-happily that word means at present another thing than artizan: with us who either practise the arts with our own hands, or who love them so wholly that we can enter into the inmost feelings of those who do,—with us it lies to deal with our last question, to stir up others to think of answering this: How shall we give people in general hope and pleasure in their daily work in such a way that in those days to come the word art *shall* be rightly understood?

Of all that I have to say to you this seems to me the most important,—that our daily and necessary work, which we could not escape if we would, which we would not forego if we could, should be human, serious, and pleasurable, not machine-like, trivial, or grievous. I call this not only the very foundation of Architecture in all senses of the word, but of happiness also in all conditions of life.

Let me say before I go further, that though I am nowise ashamed of repeating the words of men who have been before me in both senses, of time and insight I mean, I should be ashamed of letting you think that I forget their labours on which mine are founded. I know that the pith of what I am saying on this subject was set forth years ago, and for the first time by Mr. Ruskin in that chapter of the Stones of Venice, which is entitled, 'On the Nature of Gothic,' in words more clear and eloquent than any man else now living could use. So important do they seem to me that to my mind they should have been posted up in every school of art throughout the country; nay, in every associ-ation of English-speaking people which professes in any way to further the culture of mankind. But I am sorry to have to say it, my excuse for doing little more now than repeating those words is that they have been less heeded than most things which Mr. Ruskin has said: I suppose because people have been afraid of them, lest they should find the truth they express sticking so fast in their minds that it would either compel them to act on it, or confess themselves slothful and cowardly.

Nor can I pretend to wonder at that: for if people were once to accept it as true, that it is nothing but just and fair that every man's work should have some hope and pleasure always present in it, they must try to bring the change about that would make it so: and all history tells of no greater change in man's life than that would be.

Nevertheless, great as the change may be, Architecture has no prospects in civilisation unless the change be brought about: and 'tis my business to-day, I will not say to convince you of this, but to send some of you away uneasy lest perhaps it may be true; if I can manage that I shall have spoken to some purpose.

Let us see however in what light cultivated people, men not without serious thoughts about life, look at this matter, lest perchance we may seem to be beating the air only: when I have given you an example of this way of thinking, I will answer it to the best of my power, in the hopes of making some of you uneasy discontented and revolutionary.

Some few months ago I read in a paper the report of a speech made to the assembled work-people of a famous firm of manu-facturers (as they are called). The speech was a very humane and thoughtful one, spoken by one of the leaders of modern thought: the firm to whose people it was addressed was and is famous not only for successful commerce but also for the consideration and good will with which it treats its work-people, men and women. No wonder, therefore, that the speech was pleasant reading; for the tone of it was that of a man speaking to his friends who could well understand him and from whom he need hide nothing; but toward the end of it I came across a sentence, which set me a-thinking so hard, that I forgot all that had gone before. It was to this effect, and I think nearly in these very words, 'Since no man would work if it were not that he hoped by working to earn leisure': and the context showed that this was assumed as a self-evident truth.

Well, for many years I have had my mind fixed on what I in my turn regarded as an axiom which may be worded thus; No work which cannot be done without pleasure in the doing is worth doing; so you may think I was much disturbed at a grave and learned man taking such a completely different view of it with such calmness of certainty. What a little way, I thought, has all Ruskin's fire and eloquence made in driving into people so great a truth, a truth so fertile of consequences!

Then I turned the intrusive sentence over again in my mind: 'No man would work unless he hoped by working to earn leisure:' and I saw that this was another way of putting it: first, all the work of the world is done against the grain: second, what a man does in his 'leisure' is not work.

A poor bribe the hope of such leisure to supplement the other inducement to toil, which I take to be the fear of death by starvation: a poor bribe; for the most of men like those Yorkshire weavers and spinners (and the more part far worse than they) work for such a very small share of leisure that one must needs say that if all their hope be in that, they are pretty much beguiled of their hope!

So I thought, and this next, that if it were indeed true and beyond remedy, that no man would work unless he hoped by working to earn leisure, the hell of theologians was but little needed; for a thickly populated civilised country, where, you know, after all people must work at something, would serve their turn well enough. Yet again I knew that this theory of the general and necessary hatefulness of work was indeed the common one, and that all sorts of people held it, who without being monsters of insensibility grew fat and jolly nevertheless.

So to explain this puzzle, I fell to thinking of the one life of which I knew something—my own to wit—and out tumbled the bottom of the theory.

For I tried to think what would happen to me if I were forbidden my ordinary daily work; and I knew that I should die of despair and weariness, unless I could straightaway take to something else which I could make my daily work: and it was clear to me that I worked not in the least in the world for the sake of earning leisure by it, but partly driven by the fear of starvation or disgrace, and partly, and even a very great deal, because I love the work itself: and as for my leisure: well I had to confess that part of it I do indeed spend as a dog does—in contemplation, let us say; and like it well enough: but part of it also I spend in work: which work gives me just as much pleasure as my bread earning work—neither more nor less; and therefore could be no bribe or hope for my work-a-day hours.

Then next I turned my thoughts to my friends: mere artists, and therefore, you know, lazy people by prescriptive right: I found that the one thing they enjoyed was their work, and that their only idea of happy leisure was other work, just as valuable to the world as their work-a-day work: they only differed from me in liking the dog-like leisure less and the man-like labour more than I do.

I got no further when I turned from mere artists, to important men—public men: I could see no signs of their working merely to earn leisure: they all worked for the work and the deeds' sake. Do rich gentlemen sit up all night in the House of Commons for the sake of earning leisure? if so, 'tis a sad waste of labour. Or Mr. Gladstone? he doesn't seem to have succeeded in winning much leisure by tolerably strenuous work; what he does get he might have got on much easier terms, I am sure.

Does it then come to this, that there are men, say a class of men, whose daily work, though maybe they cannot escape from doing it, is chiefly pleasure to them; and other classes of men whose daily work is wholly irksome to them, and only endurable because they hope while they are about it to earn thereby a little leisure at the day's end?

If that were wholly true the contrast between the two kinds of lives would be greater than the contrast between the utmost delicacy of life and the utmost hardship could show, or between the utmost calm and the utmost trouble. The difference would be literally immeasurable.

But I dare not, if I would, in so serious a matter overstate the evils I call on you to attack: it is not wholly true that such immeasurable difference exists between the lives of divers classes of men, or the world would scarce have got through to past the middle of this century: misery, grudging, and tyranny would have destroyed us all.

The inequality even at the worst is not really so great as that: any employment in which a thing can be done better or worse has some pleasure in it, for all men do more or less like doing what they can do well: even mechanical labour is pleasant to some people (to me amongst others) if it be not too mechanical.

Nevertheless though it be not wholly true that the daily work of some men is merely pleasant and of others merely grievous: yet is it over true both that things are not very far short of this, and also that if people do not open their eyes in time they will speedily worsen? Some work, nay, almost all the work done by artizans *is* too mechanical; and those that work at it must either abstract their thoughts from it altogether, in which case they are but machines while they are at work; or else they must suffer such dreadful weariness in getting through it, as one can scarcely bear to think of. Nature, who desires that we shall at least live, but seldom, I suppose, allows this latter misery to happen; and the workmen who do purely mechanical work do as a rule become mere machines as far as their work is concerned. Now as I am quite sure that no art, not even the feeblest, rudest or least intelligent, can come of such work, so also I am sure that such work makes the workman less than a man and degrades him grievously and unjustly, and that nothing can compensate him or us for such degradation: and I want you specially to note that this was instinctively felt in the very earliest days of what are called the industrial arts. When a man turned the wheel, or threw the shuttle, or hammered the iron, he was expected to make something more than a water-pot, a cloth, or a knife, he was expected to make a work of art also: he could scarcely altogether fail in this, he might attain to making a work of the greatest beauty: this was felt to be positively necessary to the peace of mind both of the maker and the user; and this it is which I have called Architecture: the turning of necessary articles of daily use into works of art.

Certainly, when we come to think of it thus, there does seem to be little less than that immeasurable contrast above mentioned between such work and mechanical work: and most assuredly do I believe that the crafts which fashion our familiar wares need this enlightment of happiness no less now than they did in the days of the early Pharaohs: but we have forgotten this necessity, and in consequence have reduced handicraft to such degradation, that a learned, thoughtful and humane man can set forth as an axiom that no man will work except to earn leisure thereby.

But now let us forget any conventional ways of looking at the labour which produces the matters of our daily life, which ways come partly from the wretched state of the arts in modern times, and partly I suppose from that repulsion to handicraft which seems to have beset some minds in all ages: let us forget this, and try to think how it really fares with the divers ways of work in handicrafts.

I think one may divide the work with which Architecture is conversant into three classes: first there is the purely mechanical: those who do this are machines only, and the less they think of what they are doing the better for the purpose, supposing they are properly drilled: the purpose of this work, to speak plainly, is not the making of wares of any kind, but what on the one hand is called employment, on the other what is called money-making: that is to say, in other words, the multiplication of the species of the mechanical workman, and the increase of the riches of the man who sets him to work, called in our modern jargon by a strange perversion of language, a manufacturer: Let us call this kind of work Mechanical Toil.

The second kind is more or less mechanical as the case may be; but it can always be done better or worse: if it is to be well done, it claims attention from the workman, and he must leave on it signs of his individuality: there will be more or less of art in it, over which the workman has had at least some control; and he will work on it partly to earn his bread in not too toilsome or disgusting a way, but in a way which makes even his work-hours pass pleasantly to him, and partly to make wares, which when made will be a distinct gain to the world; things that will be praised and delighted in. This work I would call Intelligent Work.

The third kind of work has but little if anything mechanical about it; it is altogether individual; that is to say, that what any man does by means of it could never have been done by any other man. Properly speaking, this work is all pleasure: true, there are pains and perplexities and wearinesses in it, but they are like the troubles of a beautiful life; the dark places that make the bright ones brighter; they are the romance of the work and do but elevate the workman, not depress him: I would call this imaginative work.

Now I can fancy that at first sight it may seem to you as if there were more difference between this last and Intelligent Work, than between Intelligent Work and Mechanical Toil: but 'tis not so. The difference between these two is the difference between light and darkness, between Ormused and Ahriman: whereas the difference between Intelligent work and what for want of a better word I am calling Imaginative work, is a matter of degree only; and in times when art is abundant and noble there is no break in the chain from humblest of the lower to the greatest of the higher class: from the poor weaver who chuckles as the bright colour comes round again, to the great painter anxious and doubtful if he can give to the world the whole of his thought or only nine-tenths of it, they are all artists—that is men; while the mechanical workman, who does not note the difference between bright and dull in his colours, but only knows them by numbers, is, while he is at his work, no man, but a machine. Indeed when Intelligent work coexists with Imaginative, there is no hard and fast line between them; in the very best and happiest times of art, there is scarce any Intelligent work which is not Imaginative also; and there is but little of effort or doubt or sign of unexpressed desires even in the highest of the Imaginative work: the blessing of Equality elevates the lesser, and calms the greater art.

Now further, Mechanical Toil is bred of that hurry and thoughtlessness of civilisation of which, as aforesaid, the middle-classes of this country have been such powerful furtherers: on the face of it it is hostile to civilisation, a curse that civilisation has made for itself and can no longer think of abolishing or controlling: such it seems, I say, but since it bears with it change and tremendous change, it may well be that there is something more than mere loss in it: it will full surely destroy art as we know art, unless art newborn destroy it: yet belike at the worst it will destroy other things beside which are the poison of art, and in the long run itself also, and thus make way for the new art, of whose form we know nothing.

Intelligent work is the child of struggling, hopeful, progressive civilisation: and its office is to add fresh interest to simple and uneventful lives, to soothe discontent with innocent pleasure fertile of deeds gainful to mankind; to bless the many toiling millions with hope daily recurring, and which it will by no means disappoint.

Imaginative work is the very blossom of civilisation triumphant and hopeful; it would fain lead men to aspire towards perfection: each hope that it fulfils gives birth to yet another hope: it bears in its bosom the worth and the meaning of life and the counsel to strive to understand everything, to fear nothing and to hate nothing: in a word 'tis the symbol and sacrament of the Courage of the World.

Now thus it stands to-day with these three kinds of work: Mechanical Toil has swallowed Intelligent Work and all the lower part of Imaginative Work, and the enormous mass of the very worst now confronts the slender but still bright array of the very best: what is left of art is rallied to its citadel of the highest intellectual art, and stands at bay there.

At first sight its hope of victory is slender indeed: yet to us now living it seems as if man had not yet lost all that part of his soul which longs for beauty: nay we cannot but hope that it is not yet dying. If we are not deceived in that hope, if the art of to-day has really come alive out of the slough of despond which we call the eighteenth century, it will surely grow and gather strength, and draw to it other forms of intellect and hope that now scarcely know it; and then, whatever changes it may go through it will at the last be victorious, and bring abundant content to mankind. On the other hand, if, as some think, it be but a reflection and feeble ghost of that glorious autumn which ended the good days of the mighty art of the Middle Ages, it will take but little killing: Mechanical Toil will sweep over all the handiwork of man, and art will be gone.

I myself am too busy a man to trouble myself much as to what may happen after that: I can only say that if you do not like the thought of that dull blank, even if you know or care little for art, do not cast the thought of it aside, but think of it again and again, and cherish the trouble it breeds till such a future seems unendurable to you; and then make up your minds that you will not bear it; and even if you distrust the artists that now are, set yourself to clear the way for the artists that are to come. We shall not count you among our enemies then, however hardly you deal with us.

I have spoken of one most important part[s] of that task; I have prayed you to set yourselves earnestly to protecting what is left, and recovering what is lost of the Natural Fairness of the earth; no less I pray you to do what you may to raise up some firm ground amid the great flood of mechanical toil, to make an effort to win human and hopeful work for yourselves and your fellows.

But if our first task of guarding the beauty of the Earth was hard, this is far harder, nor can I pretend to think that we can attack our enemy directly; yet indirectly surely something may be done, or at least the foundations laid for something.

For Art breeds Art, and every worthy work done and delighted in by maker and user begets a longing for more: and since art cannot be fashioned by mechanical toil, the demand for real art will mean a demand for intelligent work, which if persisted in will in time create its due supply—at least I hope so.

I believe that what I am now saying will be well understood by those who really care about art, but to speak plainly I know that these are rarely to be found even among the cultivated classes: it must be confessed that the middle classes of our civilisation have embraced luxury instead of art, and that we are even so blindly base as to hug ourselves on it, and to insult the memory of valiant peoples of past times and to mock at them because they were not encumbered with the nuisances that foolish habit has made us look on as necessaries. Be sure that we are not beginning to prepare for the art that is to be, till we have swept all that out of our minds, and are setting to work to rid ourselves of all the useless luxuries (by some called comforts) that make our stuffy art-stifling houses more truly savage than a Zulu's kraal or an East Greenlander's snow hut.

I feel sure that many a man is longing to set his hand to this if he only durst; I believe that there are simple people who think that they are dull to art, and who are really only perplexed and wearied by finery and rubbish: if not from these, 'tis at least from the children of these that we may look for the beginnings of the building up of the art that is to be.

Meanwhile, I say, till the beginning of new construction is obvious, let us be at least destructive of the sham art: it is full surely one of the curses of modern life, that if people have not time and eyes to discern or money to buy the real object of their desire, they must needs have its mechanical substitute. On this lazy and cowardly habit feeds and grows and flourishes mechanical toil and all the slavery of mind and body it brings with it: from this stupidity are born the itch of the public to over-reach the tradesmen they deal with, the determination (usually successful) of the tradesman to over-reach them, and all the mockery and flouting that has been cast of late (not without reason) on the British tradesman and the British workman,— men just as honest as ourselves, if we would not compel them to cheat us, and reward them for doing it.

Now if the public knew anything of art, that is excellence in things made by man, they would not abide the shams of it; and if the real thing were not to be had, they would learn to do without, nor think their gentility injured by the forbearance.

Simplicity of life, even the barest, is not misery, but the very foundation of refinement: a sanded floor and whitewashed walls, and the green trees, and flowery meads, and living waters outside; or a grimy palace amid the smoke with a regiment of housemaids always working to smear the dirt together so that it may be unnoticed; which, think you, is the most refined, the most fit for a gentleman of those two dwellings?

So I say, if you cannot learn to love real art, at least learn to hate sham art and reject it. It is not so much because the wretched thing is so ugly and silly and useless that I ask you to cast it from you; it is much more because these are but the outward symbols of the poison that lies within them: look through them and see all that has gone to their fashioning, and you will see how vain labour, and sorrow, and disgrace have been their companions from the first,—and all this for trifles that no man really needs!

Learn to do without; there is virtue in those words; a force that rightly used would choke both demand and supply of Mechanical Toil: would make it stick to its last: the making of machines.

And then from simplicity of life would rise up the longing for beauty, which cannot yet be dead in men's souls, and we know that nothing can satisfy that demand but Intelligent work rising gradually into Imaginative work; which will turn all 'operatives' into workmen, into artists, into men.

Now, I have been trying to show you how the hurry of Modern Civilisation accompanied by the tyrannous organization of labour which was a necessity to the full development of Competitive Commerce, has taken from the people at large, gentle and simple, the eyes to discern and the hands to fashion that popular art which was once the chief solace and joy of the world: I have asked you to think of that as no light matter but a grievous mishap: I have prayed you to strive to remedy this evil: first by guarding jealously what is left, and by trying earnestly to win back what is lost of the Fairness of the Earth; and next by rejecting luxury, that you may embrace art, if you can, or if indeed you in your short lives cannot learn what art means, that you may at least live a simple life fit for men.

And in all I have been saying, what I have been really urging on you is this; Reverence for the life of Man upon the Earth: let the past be past, every whit of it that is not still living in us: let the dead bury their dead, but let us turn to the living, and with boundless courage and what hope we may, refuse to let the Earth by joyless in the days to come.

What lies before us of hope or fear for this? Well, let us remember that those past days whose art was so worthy, did nevertheless forget much of what was due to the Life of Man upon the Earth; and so belike it was to revenge this neglect that art was delivered to our hands for maiming: to us, who were blinded by our eager chase of those things which our forefathers had neglected, and by the chase of other things which seemed revealed to us on our hurried way, not seldom, it may be for our beguiling.

And of that to which we were blinded, not all was unworthy: nay the most of it was deep-rooted in men's souls, and was a necessary part of their Life upon the Earth, and claims our reverence still: let us add this knowledge to our other knowledge, and there will still be a future for the arts. Let us remember this, and amid simplicity of life turn our eyes to real beauty that can be shared by all: and then though the days worsen, and no rag of the elder art be left for our teaching, yet the new art may yet arise among us: and even if it have the hands of a child together with the heart of a troubled man, still it may bear on for us to better times the tokens of our reverence for the Life of Man upon the Earth. For we indeed freed from the bondage of foolish habit and dulling luxury might at last have eyes wherewith to see: and should have to babble to one another many things of our joy in the life around us: the faces of people in the streets bearing the tokens of mirth and sorrow and hope, and all the tale of their lives: the scraps of nature the busiest of us would come across; birds and beasts and the little worlds they live in; and even in the very town the sky above us and the drift of the clouds across it; the wind's hand on the slim trees, and its voice amid their branches, and all the ever-recurring deeds of nature: nor would the road or the river winding past our homes fail to tell us stories of the country-side, and men's doings in field and fell. And whiles we should fall to muse on the times when all the ways of nature were mere wonders to men, yet so well beloved of them that they called them by men's names and gave them deeds of men to do: and many a time there would come before us memories of the deeds of past times, and of the aspirations of those mighty peoples whose deaths have made our lives, and their sorrows our joys.

How could we keep silence of all this? and what voice could

tell it but the voice of art: and what audience for such a tale would content us but all men living on the earth?

This is what Architecture hopes to be: it will have this life, or else death; and it is for us now living between the past and the future to say whether it shall live or die.

Notes

1   The Kyrle Society was constituted in 1875 as the Society for the Diffusion of Beauty by Miranda Hill, sister of the noted housing reformer. A special 'decorative branch' of the Society was established in 1879. Chaired by the architect C.H. Townsend, it was vigorously supported by Morris. The Commons Preservation Society was founded on 19 July 1865 in the chambers of George Shaw Lefevre. Its greatest early triumph came in 1874, when it succeeded in preventing the enclosure and development of the remains of Epping Forest. See G. Murphy, *Founders of the National Trust* (London: Christopher Helm, 1987), pp. 11-13, 25-36.

2   In summer 1881 Morris and the Society for the Protection of Ancient Buildings fought proposals to widen Magdalen Bridge, Oxford. The work was necessary to accommodate a new tram line. By December 1881 it was clear that the SPAB campaign had failed. See Kelvin (ed.), *Collected Letters*, II, pp. 55-7, 74, 77-9, 85-6.

ARCHITECTURE AND HISTORY

1884

W e of this Society at least know the beauty of the weathered and time-worn surface of an ancient building, and have all of us felt the grief of seeing this surface disappear under the hands of a "restorer;" but though we all feel this deeply enough, some of us perhaps may be puzzled to explain to the outside world the full value of this ancient surface. It is not merely that it is in itself picturesque and beautiful, though that is a great deal; neither is it only that there is a sentiment attaching to the very face which the original builders gave their work, but dimly conscious all the while of the many generations which should gaze on it; it is only a part of its value that the stones are felt to be, as Mr. Ruskin beautifully puts it, speaking of some historic French building, now probably changed into an academic model of its real self, that they are felt to be "the very stones which the eyes of St. Louis saw lifted into their places." That sentiment is much, but is not all; nay, it is but a part of the especial value to which I wish to-day to call your attention, which value briefly is, that the untouched surface of ancient architecture bears witness to the development of man's ideas, to the continuity of history, and, so doing, affords never-ceasing instruction, nay education, to the passing generations, not only telling us what were the aspirations of men passed away, but also what we may hope for in the time to come.

You all know what a different spirit has animated history in

these latter days from that which used to be thought enough to
give it interest to thinking men. Time was, and not so long ago,
when the clever essay writer (rather than historian) made his
history surrounded by books whose value he weighed rather by
the degree in which they conformed to an arbitrary standard of
literary excellence, than by any indications they might give of
being able to afford a glimpse into the past. So treated, the very
books were not capable of yielding the vast stores of knowledge
of history which they really possessed, if dealt with by the
historical method. It is true that for the most part these books
were generally written for other purposes than that of giving
simple information to those to come after; at their honestest the
writers were compelled to look on life through the spectacles
thrust on them by the conventional morality of their own times;
at their *dishonestest*, they were servile flatterers in the pay of the
powers that were. Nevertheless, though the art of lying has
always been sedulously cultivated by the world, and especially by
that part of it which lives on the labour of others, it is an art
which few people attain to in its perfection, and the honest man
by the use of sufficient diligence can generally manage to see
through the veil of sophistry into the genuine life which exists in
those written records of the past; nay, the very lies themselves,
being for the most part of a rough and simple nature, can often
be dissolved and precipitated, so to say, into historical substance,
into negative evidence of facts.

But the academical historians of whom I have spoken were
not fitted for the task; they themselves were cursed with a fatal
though unconscious dishonesty; the world of history which they
pictured to themselves was an unreal one; to them there were but
two periods of continuous order, of organised life: the period of
Greek and Roman classical history was one, the time from the
development of the retrospection into that period till their own
days was the other; all else to them was mere accidental confusion, strange tribes and clans with whom they had no relation,

jostling against one another for no purpose save that of a herd of bisons; all the thousands of years devoid of creation, laden only with mere obstruction, and out of that, as I said, two periods of perfection, leaping fully equipped like Pallas from the brain of Zeus. A strange conception, truly, of the history of the "famous men and our fathers that begat us," but one which could not hold out long against the natural development of knowledge and society. The mists of pedantry slowly lifted and showed a different picture; inchoate order in the remotest times, varying indeed among different races and countries, but swayed always by the same laws, moving forward ever towards something that seems the very opposite of that which it started from, and yet the earlier order never dead but living in the new, and slowly moulding it to a recreation of its former self. How different a spirit such a view of history must create it is not difficult to see. No longer shallow mockery at the failures and follies of the past, from a standpoint of so-called civilisation, but deep sympathy with its half-conscious aims, from amidst the difficulties and shortcomings that we are only too sadly conscious of to-day; that is the new spirit of history; knowledge I would fain think has brought us humility, and humility hope of that perfection which we are obviously so far short of.

Now, further, as to the instruments of this new knowledge of history, were they not chiefly two: study of language and study of archaeology?[1] that, is of the expression of men's ideas by means of speech, and by means of handiwork, in other words the record of man's creative deeds. Of the first of these instruments, deeply as I am interested in it, and especially on the side which, tending towards comparative mythology, proclaims so clearly the unity of mankind, of this I lack the knowledge to speak, even if I had the time; on the second, archaeology, I am bound to speak, as it is above all things the function of our Society to keep before people's eyes its importance as an instrument of the study of history, which does in very truth lead us towards the solution of all the social and political problems over which men's minds are busied.

I am all the more bound to speak on this subject because, in spite of the ascendency which the new spirit of history has over cultivated minds, we must not forget that many minds are uncultivated, and in them the pedantic spirit still bears sway; and you will understand that when I speak of uncultivated minds, I am not thinking of the lower classes, as we civilly, but too truly, call them, but of many of those who are in responsible positions, and responsible especially as to the guardianship of our ancient buildings; indeed, to meet one conceivable objection, I can understand a man saying that the half-ignorant, half-instructed, and wholly pedantic way of dealing with an ancient building is historical also, and I can admit some logic in the objection; destruction is, alas! one of the forms of growth; indeed those pedantic historians I have been speaking of had their share also in history, and it is a curious question, which I cannot follow at present, as to how far their destructive pedantry was a sign of strength as compared with our reasonable research and timidity; I say that I cannot follow this question up, though I think it would lead to conclusions astonishing to some people, and so will content myself with saying that if the narrowness, the vulgarity of mind (I know no other word), which deals with our ancient monuments, as if Art had no past and is to have no future, be an historical development (and I don't gainsay it), so also is the spirit which animates us to resist that vulgarity—"for this among the rest was I ordained."

Now, I am sure that, so far I have carried you with me as members of our Society; you cannot doubt that in one way or other the surface of an ancient building, the *handling* of the old handicraftsman that is, is most valuable and worthy of preservation, and I am sure also that we all feel instinctively that it cannot be reproduced at the present day; that the attempt at reproduction not only deprives us of a monument of history, but also of a work of art. In what follows I have to attempt the task of showing you that this impossibility of reproduction is not accidental, but is essential to the conditions of life at the present day; that it is caused by the results of all past history, and not by a passing taste or fashion of the time; and that consequently no man, and no body of men, however learned they may be in ancient art, whatever skill in design or love of beauty they may have, can persuade, or bribe, or force our workmen of to-day to do their work in the same way as the workmen of Kind Edward I, did theirs. Wake up Theoderic the Goth from his sleep of centuries, and place him on the throne of Italy; turn our modern House of Commons into the Witenagemote (or meeting of the *wise* men) of King Alfred the Great; no less a feat is the restoration of an ancient building.

Now, in order to show you that this is necessary and inevitable, I am compelled very briefly to touch upon the conditions under which handiwork has been produced from the classical times onward; in doing so I cannot avoid touching on certain social problems, on the solution of which some of you may differ from me. In that case I ask you to remember that though the Committee has ordered me to read this paper to you, it cannot be held responsible for any opinions outside the principles advocated in its published documents. The Society should not be regarded as *dangerous*, except, perhaps, to the amusements of certain country parsons and squires, and their wives and daughters.

Well, it must be admitted that every architectural work is a work of co-operation. The very designer, be he never so original, pays his debt to this necessity in being in some form or another under the influence of *tradition*; dead men guide his hand even when he forgets that they ever existed. But, furthermore, he must get his ideas carried out by other men; no man can build a building with his own hands; every one of those men depends for the possibility of even beginning his work on someone else;

each one is but part of a machine; the parts may be but machines themselves, or they may be intelligent, but in either case must work in subordination to the general body. It is clear that men so working must be influenced in their work by their conditions of life, and the man who organises their labour must make up his mind that he can only get labour of a kind which those conditions have bred. To expect enthusiasm for good workmanship from men who for two generations have been accustomed by the pressure of circumstances to work slovenly would be absurd; to expect consciousness of beauty from men who for ten generations have not been allowed to produce beauty, more absurd still. The workmanship of every piece of co-operative work must belong to its period, and be characteristic of it. Understand this clearly, which I now put in another form: all architectural work must be co-operative; in all co-operative work the finished wares can be no better in quality than the lowest, or simplest, or widest grade, which is also the most essential, will allow them to be. The kind and quality of that work, the work of the ordinary handicraftsman, is determined by the social conditions under which he lives, which differ much from age to age.

Let us then try to see how they have differed, and glance at the results to Art of that difference; during which inquiry we shall have much more to do with the developed Middle Ages, with the work of which our Society is chiefly concerned, than with any other period.

In the classical period industrial production was chiefly carried on by slaves, whose persons and work alike belonged to their employers, and who were sustained at just such standard of life as suited the interests of the said employers. It was natural that under these circumstances industrialism should be despised, but under Greek civilisation, at least, ordinary life for the free citizens, the aristocracy in fact, was simple, the climate was not exacting of elaborate work for the purposes of clothing and shelter, the race was yet young, vigorous, and physically beautiful.

The aristocracy, therefore, freed from the necessity of rough and exhausting work by their possession of chattel slaves, who did all that for them, and little oppressed with anxieties for their livelihood, had, in spite of the constant brawling and piracy which forms their external history, both inclination and leisure to cultivate the higher intellectual arts within the limits which their natural love of matter of fact and hatred of romance prescribed to them; the lesser arts, meantime, being kept in rigid, and indeed slavish subordination to them as was natural. May I break off here to ask you to consider, in case any Athenian gentlemen had attempted to build a Gothic cathedral in the days of Pericles, what sort of help he would have had from the slave labour of the day, and what kind of Gothic they would have produced for him?

Well, the ideal of art established by the intellect of the Greeks with such splendid and overwhelming success lasted throughout the whole Roman period also, in spite of the invention and use of the arch in architecture, or rather in building; and side by side with it chattel slavery, under somewhat changed conditions, produced the ordinary wares of life; the open-mouthed contempt for the results of industrial production expressed by the pedant Pliny, whether it were genuine or artificially deduced from the conventionalities of philosophy, well illustrates the condition of the slave-produced lesser arts of the later classical period.

Meantime, and while Pliny was alive, the intellectual arts of classical times had long fallen from their zenith, and had to wade through weary centuries of academicalism, from which they were at last redeemed by no recurrence of individual genius to the earlier and human period, but by the break-up of classical society itself; which involved the change of chattel slavery, the foundation of classical society, into serfdom or villeinage, on which the feudal system was based. The period of barbarism or disorder between the two periods of order was long doubtless, but the new order rose out of it at last bright and clear; and in place of the system of aristocratic citizens and chattel slave without rights dominated by the worship of the city, which was the ideal, the religion of classic society, was formed a system of personal duties and rights, personal service and protection in subordination to *a priori* ideas of mankind's duties to and claims from the unseen powers of the universe. No doubt, as was natural in this hierarchical system, the religious houses, whose distinct duty it was to hold the hierarchical ideal up as a banner amongst imperfect men, fulfilled towards the arts in the earlier Middle Ages, amidst the field-serfs and their lords, the function which in classical times the cultivated Greek free man fulfilled amidst his crowd of enslaved menials. But the serf was in a very different condition from the chattel slave; for, certain definite duties being performed for his lord, he was (in theory at least) at liberty to earn his living as he best could within the limits of his manor. The chattel slave, as an individual, had the hope of manumission, but collectively there was no hope for him but in the complete and mechanical overturn of the society which was founded on his subjection. The serf, on the other hand, was, by the conditions of his labour, forced to strive to better himself as an individual, and collectively soon began to acquire rights amidst the clashing rights of king, lord, and burgher. Also, quite early in the Middle Ages, a new and mighty force began to germinate for the help of labour, the first signs of secular combination among free men, producers, and distributors.

The *guilds*, whose first beginning in England dates from before the Norman Conquest, although they fully recognised the hierarchical conditions of society, and were indeed often in early times mainly religious in their aims, did not spring from ecclesiasticism, nay, in all probability, had their roots in that part of the European race which had not known of Rome and her institutions in the days of her temporal domination. England and Denmark were the foremost countries in the development of the guilds, which took root latest and most feebly in the Latinised countries.

The spirit of combination spread; the guilds, which at first had been rather benefit societies or clubs than anything else, soon developed into bodies for the protection and freedom of commerce, and rapidly became powerful under the name of merchant guilds; in the height of their power there formed under them another set of guilds, whose object was the regulation and practice of the crafts in freedom from feudal exactions. The older merchant guilds resisted these newer institutions; so much so that in Germany there was bloody and desperate war between them; the great revolt of Ghent, you will remember as an illustration of this hostility, was furthered by the lesser crafts, as Froissart[2] calls them; and again remember that Ghent, the producing city, was revolutionary, Bruges, the commercial one, reactionary. In England the merchant guilds changed in a more peaceable manner, and became in the main the corporations of the towns, and the craft-guilds took their definite place as regulators and protectors of all handicrafts. By the beginning of the fourteenth century the supremacy of the craft-guilds was complete, and at that period at least their constitution was thoroughly democratic; mere journeymen there were none, the apprentices were sure, as a matter of course, to take their places as masters of their craft when they learned it.

Now before we go on to consider the decline and fall of the guilds, let us look at the way in which the craftsman worked at that period: and first a word as to his conditions of life: for I must tell you very briefly that he lived, however roughly, yet at least far easier than his successor does now. He worked for no master save the public, he made his wares from beginning to end himself, and sold them himself to the man who was going to use them. This was the case at least with nearly all, if not all, the goods made in England; some of the rarer goods, such as silk cloth, did come into the chaffering market, which had to be the case all the more for this, that the materials of any country were chiefly wrought into goods close to their birthplace. But even in the cases of these rarer goods they were made primarily for home consumption, and only the overplus came into the hands of the merchant; concerning which latter you must also remember that he was not a mere gambler in the haphazard of supply and demand as he is today, but an indispensable distributor of goods; he was paid for his trouble in bringing goods from a place where there was more than was needed of them to a country where there was not enough, and that was all; the laws against forestallers and regratters give an idea of how this matter of commerce was looked on in the Middle Ages, as commerce, viz, not profitmongering. A forestaller was a man who bought up produce to hold it for a rise, a regratter, a man who bought and sold in the same market or within five miles of it. On the advantages of the forestaller to the community it is scarcely necessary to dwell, I think: as to the regratter, it was the view of the benighted people of the Middle Ages that a man who bought, say, a hundred-weight of cheese for 2d. a pound at nine in the morning and sold it at eleven for 3d. was not a specially useful citizen. I confess I am sufficiently old-fashioned and conservative to agree with them on that head, although I cannot help perceiving that all "business," properly so called, is now forestalling and regratting, and that we are all the slaves of those delightful and simple professions—so that the criminals of one age have become the benevolent masters of the next.

Well, anyhow, it followed from this direct intercourse between the maker and the consumer of goods, that the public in general were good judges of manufactured wares, and, in consequence, that the art, or religion rather, of adulteration was scarcely known; at least, it was easy to win the fame of a confessor, if not a martyr, of that noble creed.

Now, as to the manner of work, there was little or no division of labour in each craft; that I think is some mitigation of the evil—for I look upon it as such, of a man being bound down to one craft for his life long (as he is now also)—some mitigation, because, after all, there was plenty of variety in the work of a man who made the whole of a piece of goods himself, instead of making always one little piece of a piece. Also you must note that the freemen of the guilds had their share in the pasture lands of the country, as every free man at least had. Port Meadow, at Oxford, for instance, was the communal pasture of the freemen of that city.

These were the conditions of life and work of the English craftsmen of the fourteenth century. I suppose most of us have declined to accept the picture of him which we have had presented to us by the half ignorant and wholly misleading pedants of whom I have spoken before. We who have studied the remains of his handicrafts have been, without any further research, long instinctively sure that he was no priest-ridden, down-trodden savage, but a thoughtful and vigorous man, and in some sense, at least, *free*. That instinct has been abundantly confirmed by painstaking collectors of facts, like Mr. Thorold Rogers,[3] and we now know that the guild craftsman led the sort of life in work and play that we should have expected from the art he produced. He worked, not for the profit of a master, but for his own livelihood, which, I repeat, he did not find it difficult to earn, so that he had a good deal of leisure, and being master of his time, his tools, and his material, was not bound to turn out his work shabbily, but could afford to amuse himself by giving it artistic finish; how different that is from mechanical or trade finish some of us, at least, have learned—maybe, by the way of Weeping Cross. Well, that artistic finish or ornament was not venal, it was given freely to the public, who, I rather think, paid for it by interest in and sympathy for the work itself, which, indeed, I consider a good payment in times when a man could live otherwise without payment more gross and material. For here I must make the confession that what is called in modern slang the "wages of genius," were much neglected by the builders of our ancient buildings; for art, as Mr. Thorold Rogers justly says, was widespread; the possession of some skill in it was the rule and not the exception. As a rule, those who could afford to pay for a building, were able to do the necessary planning and designing, obviously because they would naturally find help and harmonious intelligence among the men they had to employ. For instance, the tower of Merton College Chapel at Oxford was carried out by ordinary masons, under the superintendence of the Fellows of the College. Well, judging from the wretched tinkering that the present Fellows have allowed to be perpetrated on their beautiful succursal house, St. Albans' Hall, I would not venture to trust the present most respectable Fellows of that ancient House with such a job now.

So it followed from this widespread skill in the arts, that those poor wretches who had skill and taste beyond their fellow-workman, and who in consequence had pleasanter work than they, had to put up with a very moderate additional wage, and in some cases with nothing additional; it seems they could not make good the claim now preferred for that much sinned against—and much sinning—company, men of genius, that the conformation of their stomachs and the make of their skin is different from that of other men, and that consequently they want more to eat and drink and different raiment from their fellows. In most sober earnest, when we hear it said, as it often is said, that extra money payment is necessary under all circumstances to produce great works of art, and that men of special talent will not use those talents without being bribed by mere gross material advantages, we, I say, shall know what to reply. We can appeal to the witness of those lovely works still left to us, whose unknown, unnamed creators were content to give them to the world, with little more extra wages than what their pleasure in their work and their sense of usefulness in it might bestow on them.

Well, I must now say that it seems to me that a body of artificers, so living as we have seen, and so working, with simple machines or instruments, of which they were complete masters, had very great advantages for the production of architectural art, using that word at its widest; and that one would, reasoning *a priori*, expect to find in their work that thoughtfulness and fertility of resource that blended freedom and harmonious co-operation, which, as a matter of fact, we do find in it. Nevertheless, in spite of this free intelligence of the mediaeval workman, or even because of it, he was still compelled to work only as tradition would allow him to do. If it could ever have occurred to any man's mind to build some new Parthenon or Erectheum by the banks of Thames, or Warfe, or Wensum, in the fourteenth century, how far do you think his fellow-workman's skill would have been able to second his folly?

But we must leave the fourteenth century awhile, and hurry on in our tale of the workman's lot. I have said that the constitution of the craft guild was at first thoroughly democratic or fraternal, but it did not long remain so. As the towns grew bigger and population flowed to them from the enfranchised field-serfs and other sources, the old craftsmen began to form a separate and privileged class in the guilds with their privileged apprentices, and the journeyman at last made his appearance. After a while the journeymen attempted to form guilds under the master crafts, as the latter had done under the merchant guilds; but the economic conditions of the time tending now more and more towards manufacturing for a profit, beat them, and they failed. Nevertheless, the conditions of work did not change much, the masters were checked by laws in favour of the journeymen, and wages rather rose than fell all through the fifthteenth century; nor did division of labour begin till much later; everywhere the artisan was still an artist.

The beginning of the great change came with the Tudors in the first quarter of the sixteenth century, during which time England, from being a country of tillage cultivated for livelihood, became a grazing country farmed for profit. He who runs may read the tale of this change and its miseries in the writings of

More and Latimer. All I need say about it here is, that it had a
very direct influence upon the conditions of life and manner of
work of the artisans, for the crafts were now flooded by the
crowds of landless men, who had nothing but the force of their
bodies to live upon, and were obliged to sell that force day by day
for what those would give them who certainly would not buy the
article labour unless they could make a profit by it. The brutal
rapine with which the change of religion in England was carried
out; the wanton destruction of our public buildings which
accompanied the stealing of our public lands, doubtless played its
part in degrading what art was still possible under the new conditions of labour.

But the Reformation itself was but one of the aspects of the
new spirit of the time produced by great economical changes,
and which dealt with art and its creator, labour, far more completely than any series of accidents could do, however momentous they might be. The change in the conditions of labour went
on speedily, though there was still a good deal of what may be
called domestic manufacture; the workmen in the towns got to
be more dependent on their employers, more and more mere
journeymen, and a great change was coming over the manner of
their work; the mere collection of them into big workshops
under one master, in itself merely gave economy of space, rent,
fire, lighting, and the rest, but it was the prelude to a much
greater change; division of labour now began, and speedily
gained head. Under the old mediaeval conditions the unit of
labour was a master craftsman who knew his business from
beginning to end; such help as he had was from mere apprentices
who were learning their business, and were not doomed to life-
long service. But with the new system of master and men came
this change, that the unit of production was a group, each
member of which depended on every one of the others, and was
helpless without them. Under this system, called the division of
labour system, a man may be, and often is condemned for the

whole of his life to make the insignificant portion of an insignificant article of the market. I use the present tense, because this
system of division of labour is still going on side by side with the
last development of manufacturing for profit, of which more
anon.

Now, it is necessary for you to understand that the birth and
growth of this division of labour system was no mere accident,
was not the result, I mean, of some passing and inexplicable
fashion which caused men to desire the kind of work which
could be done by such means; it was caused by the economical
changes which forced men to produce no longer for a livelihood
as they used to do, but for a profit. Almost all goods, all except
those made in the most domestic way, had now to go through the
market before they reached the users' hands. They were made for
sale, not primarily for use, and when I say "they," I mean the
whole of them; the art in them as well as their mere obvious
utility was now become a marketable article, doled out according
to the necessities of the capitalist who employed both machine-
workman and designer, fettered by the needs of profit; for by this
time, you understand, the division of labour had so worked, that
instead of all workmen being artists, as they once were, they were
divided into workmen who were not artists, and artists who were
not workmen.

This change was complete, or nearly so, by the middle of the
eighteenth century: it is not necessary for me to trace the gradual
degradation of the arts from the fifteenth century to this point.
Suffice it to say that it was steady and certain; only where men
were more or less outside the great stream of civilisation, where
life was rude, and production wholly domestic, did the art
produced retain any signs of human pleasure: elsewhere pedantry
reigned supreme. The picture-painters who were wont to show
us, as through windows opened by them, the longings and lives
of the saints and heroes, nay, the very heavens and city of God
hanging over the earthly city of their love, were turned, what few

of them were aught else than pretentious daubers, into courtly
flatterers of ill-favoured fine ladies and stupid supercilious lords.
As for the architectural arts, what could you expect to get of them
from a set of human machines, co-operating indeed, but only for
speed and precision of production, and designed for at best by
pedants who despised the life of man, and at worst by mechanical
drudges, little better in any way than the luckless workmen?
Whatever might be expected, nothing was got but that mass of
foolish toys and costly ministrations to luxury and ostentation,
which has since those days been most worthily contemned under
the name of upholstery.

Is that the end of the story of the degradation of the arts? No,
there is another act to the drama; worse or better according as to
whether you are contented to accept it as final, or have been
stimulated to discontent, that is, hope for something better. I
have told you how the workman was reduced to a machine, I
have still to tell you how he has been pushed down from even
that giddy eminence of self-respect.

At the close of the eighteenth century England was a country
that manufactured among other countries that manufactured: her
manufactures were still secondary to her merely country life, and
were mixed up with it; in fifty years all that was changed, and
England was the manufacturing country of the world—the
workshop of the world, often so called with much pride by her
patriotic sons. Now this strange and most momentous revolution
was brought about by the machinery which the chances and
changes of the world, too long a tale even to hint at here, *forced*
on our population. You must think of this great machine industry
as though on the one hand merely the full development of the
effects of producing for profit instead of livelihood, which began
in Sir Thomas More's time, yet on the other as a revolutionary
change from that of the mere division of labour. The exigencies
of my own work have driven me to dig pretty deeply into the
strata of the eighteenth century workshop system, and I could

clearly see how very different it is from the factory system of to-day, with which it is commonly confounded; therefore it was with a ready sympathy that I read the full explanation of the change and its tendencies in the writings of a man, I will say a great man, whom, I suppose, I ought not to name in this company, and who cleared my mind on several points (also unmentionable here) relating to this subject of labour and its products. But this at least I must say, that whereas under the eighteenth-century division of labour system, a man was compelled to work for ever at a trifling piece of work in a base mechanical way, which, also, in that base way he understood, under the system of the factory and almost automatic machine under which we now live, he may change his work often enough, may be shifted from machine to machine, and scarcely know that he is producing anything at all: in other words, under the eighteenth-century system he was reduced to a machine; under that of the present day he is the slave to a machine. It is the machine which bids him what to do on pain of death by starvation. Yes, and by no means metaphorically so; the machine, for instance, can, if it pleases, if it chooses to hurry, make him walk thirty miles a day instead of twenty, and send him to the workhouse if he refuses.

Now if you ask me ('tis a by question) which is the worst off, the machine workman of the eighteenth century or the slave to the machine of the nineteenth, I am bound to say that I think the former is. If I gave you my reasons, few of you would agree with me, and I am not sure that you would allow me to finish this discourse: at any rate they are somewhat complicated. But the question as to which set of workmen produced the better work can be answered with little complication. The machine workman had to be well skilled in his contemptible task at least, the slave to the machine needs but little skill, and, as a matter of fact, his place has been taken by women and children, and what skill is needed in the work goes in the overlooking of the labours of these latter. In short, the present system of the factory and its dominating machine tends to doing away with skilled labour altogether.

Here, then, is a strange contrast, which I most seriously invite you to consider, between the craftsman of the Middle Ages and him of to-day. The mediaeval man sets to work at his own time, in his own house; probably makes his tool, instrument, or simple machine himself, even before he gets on to his web, or his lump of clay, or what not. What ornament there shall be on his finished work he himself determined, and his mind and hand designs it and carries it out; tradition, that is to say the minds and thoughts of all workmen gone before, this, in its concrete form of the customer of his craft, does indeed guide and help him; otherwise he is free. Nor must we forget that even if he lives in a town, the fields and sweet country come close up to his house, and he at whiles occupies himself in working in them, and more than once or twice in his life he has had to take the bow or brown-bill from the wall, and run his chance of meeting the great secret face to face in the ranks of battle; oftenest, indeed, in other mens' quarrels, yet sometimes in his own, nor wholly unsuccessfully then.

But he who has taken his place, how does he work and live? Something of that we all know. There he has to be at the factory-gates by the time the bell rings, or he is fined or "sent to grass." Nay, not always will the factory-gate open to him; unless the master, controlled himself by a market of which he knows little and the hand nothing, allows him space to work in and a machine to work at, he must turn back and knock about the streets, as many thousands are doing to-day in England. But suppose him there, happy before his machine; up and down he has to follow it, day in, day out, and what thoughts he has must be given to something else than his work. I repeat, 'tis as much as he can do to know what thing the machine (not he) is making. Design and ornament, what has he to do with that? Why, he may be tending a machine which makes a decent piece of work, or, on the other hand, may be an accomplice (a very small one) in turning out a blatant piece of knavery and imposture; he will get as much wages for one as the other, nor will one or the other be in the least degree within his control. All the religion, morality, philanthropy, and freedom of the nineteenth century, will not help him to escape that disgrace. Need I say how and where he lives? Lodged in a sweltering dog-hole, with miles and miles of similar dog-holes between him and the fair fields of the country, which in grim mockery is called "his". Sometimes on holidays, bundled out by train to have a look at it, to be bundled into his grimy hell again in the evening. Poor wretch!

Tell me, then, at what period of this man's working life will you pick him up and set him to imitating the work of the free crafts-guildsman of the fourteenth century, and expect him to turn out work like his in quality?

Well, not to weaken my argument by exaggeration, I admit that though a huge quantity of would-be artistic work is done by this slave of the machine at the bidding of some ridiculous market or other, the crafts relating to building have not reached that point in the industrial revolution; they are an example of my assertion that the eighteenth-century division of labour system still exists, and works side by side with the great factory and machine system. Yet here, too, the progress of the degradation is obvious enough, since the similar craftsmen of the eighteenth-century still had lingering among them scraps of tradition from the times of art now lost, while now in those crafts the division of labour system has eaten deep from the architect to the hodman, and, moreover, the standard of excellence, so far from its bearing any relation to that of the free workman of the guilds, has sunk far below that of the man enslaved by division of labour in the eighteenth century, and is not a whit better than that of the shoddy-maker of the great industries; in short, the workman of the great machine industry is the type of labour to-day.

Surely it is a curious thing that while we are ready to laugh at the idea of the possibility of the Greek workman turning out a Gothic building, or a Gothic workman turning out a Greek one, we see nothing preposterous in the Victorian workman producing a Gothic one. And this, although we have any amount of specimens of the work of the Renaissance period, whose workmen, under the pedantic and retrospective direction of the times, were theoretically supposed to be able to imitate the ancient classical work, which imitation, as a matter of fact, turned out obstinately characteristic of their own period, and derived all the merit it has from those characteristics—a curious thing, and perhaps of all the signs of weakness of art at the present day one of the most discouraging. I may be told, perhaps, that the very historical knowledge, of which I have spoken above, and which the pedantry of the Renaissance and eighteenth-century lacked, has enabled us to perform that miracle of raising the dead centuries to life again; but to my mind it is a strange view to take of historical knowledge and insight, that it should set us on the adventure of trying to retrace our steps towards the past, rather than give us some glimmer of insight into the future; a strange view of the continuity of history, that it should make us ignore the very changes which are the essence of that continuity. In truth, the art of the past cycle, that of the Renaissance, which flickered out at last in the feeble twaddle of the dilettantism of the latter Georges, had about it, as I hinted above, a supercilious confidence in itself, which entirely forbade it to accept any imitation of style but one, as desirable, which one was that which it regarded as part of itself. It could make no more choice in style than Greek or Gothic art could; it fully, if tacitly, admitted the evolution of history, accepted the division-of-labour workman, and so, indeed, did its best, and had a kind of life about it, dreary as that life was, and expressive enough of the stupid but fearless middle class domination which was the essence of the period.

But we, I say, we refuse to admit the evolution of history. We set our slave to the machine to do the work of the free mediaeval workman or of the man of the transition period indifferently. We, if no age else, have learnt the trick of masquerading in other men's cast-off clothes, and carry on a strange hypocritical theatrical performance, rather with timid stolidity than with haughty confidence, determined to shut our eyes to everything seriously disagreeable, nor heeding the silent movement of real history which is still going on around and underneath our raree show.

Surely such a state of things is a token of change—of change, speedy perhaps, complete certainly; of the visible end of one cycle and the beginning of another. For, strange to say, here is a society which on its cultivated surface has no distinct character-istics of its own, but floats, part of it hither, part thither—this set of minds drifting toward the beauty of the past, that toward the logic of the future, each tacitly at least believing that they need but count of heads on their side to establish a convention of many, which should rule the world, despite of history and logic, ignoring *necessity* which has made even their blind feebleness what it is. And all the while beneath this cultivated surface works the great commercial system, which the cultivated look on as their servant and the bond of society, but which really is their master and the breaker-up of society; for it is in itself and in its essence a war, and can only change its character with its death: man against man, class against class, with this motto, What I gain you lose, that war must go on till the great change comes whose end is peace and not war.

And what are we, who are met together here after seven years of humble striving for existence, for leave to do something? Mere straws in that ocean of half-conscious hypocrisy which is called cultivated society? Nay, I hope not. At least, we do not turn round on history and say. This is bad and that is good; I like this and I don't like that; but rather we say, This was life, and these, the works of our fathers, are material signs of it. That life lives in you, though you have forgotten it; those material signs of it, though you do not heed them, will one day be sought for: and that necessity which is even now forming the society of the time to be, and shall one day make it manifest, has amongst other things forced us to do our best to treasure them, these tokens of life past and present. The society of to-day, anarchical as it is, is nevertheless forming a new order of which we in common with all those who, I will say it, have courage to accept realities and reject shams, are and must be, a part; so that in the long run our work, hopeless as it must sometimes seem to us, will not be utterly lost. For, after all, what is it that we are contending for? The reality of art, that is to say, of the pleasure of the human race. The tendency of the commercial or competitive society, which has been developing for more than 300 years, has been towards the destruction of the pleasure of life. But that competitive society has at last developed itself so far that, as I have said, its own change and death is approaching, and as one token of the change the destruction of the pleasure of life is beginning to seem to many of us no longer a necessity but a thing to be striven against. On the genuineness and reality of that hope the existence, the reason for existence of our Society depends. Believe me, it will not be possible for a small knot of cultivated people to keep alive an interest in the art and records of the past amidst the present conditions of a sordid and heart-breaking struggle for existence for the many, and a languid sauntering through life for the few. But when society is so reconstituted that all citizens will have a chance of leading a life made up of due leisure and reasonable work, then will all society, and not our "Society" only, resolve to protect ancient buildings from all damage, wanton or accidental, for then at last they will begin to understand that they are part of their present lives, and in part of themselves. That will come when the time is ripe for it; for at present even if they knew of their loss they could not prevent it, since they are living in a state of war, that is to say, of blind waste.

Surely we of this Society have had this truth driven home practically often enough, and often had to confess that if the destruction or brutification of an ancient monument of art and history was "a matter of money," it was hopeless striving against it. Do not let us be so feeble or cowardly as to refuse to face this fact, for, for us also, although our function in forming the future of society may be a humble one, there is no compromise. Let us admit that we are living in the time of barbarism betwixt two periods of order, the order of the past and the order of the future, and then, though there may be some of us who think (as I do) that the end of that barbarism is drawing near, and others that it is far distant, yet we can both of us, I the hopeful and you the unhopeful, work together to preserve what relics of the old order are yet left us for the instruction, the pleasure, the hope of the new. So may the times of present war be less disastrous, if but a little—the times of coming peace more fruitful.

Notes

1   Morris is here referring to the Oxford School of historians. See M. Swenarton, *Artisans and Architects. The Ruskinian Tradition in Architectural Thought* (London: Macmillan Press, 1989), p. 67.

2   Jean Froissart (1337?–1405?), a French chronicler and poet who visited England in 1361 and again in 1394–5. Though sometimes unreliable, his *Chronicles* covering the period 1325–1400 remain an important source of information about the Hundred Years War and the Peasants' Revolt of 1381.

3   James Edwin Thorold Rogers (1823–90) was a radical political economist and historian who carried out ground-breaking research into the history of agriculture and prices between 1866 and 1902. Paul Meier has argued that Rogers's works exercised a profound influence on Morris's conception of the Middle Ages, possibly shaping 'A Dream of John Ball' (*Commonweal*, 1886–7). See *William Morris: The Marxist Dreamer*, translated by Frank Gubb (Sussex: Harvester Press, 1978), I, p. 110.

THE HOUSING OF THE POOR

1884

L et us on this matter be sure of one thing that as long as there are *poor* people they will be poorly housed; those of our philanthropists who have really dealt with the subject practically have no doubt about that; and consequently all their endeavours are turned to one end, trying namely to get the "poor" a little less disgracefully housed than they are at present; what they hope to accomplish is very little indeed, and they are so well aware of the difficulties of their accomplishing even this little, that they are terrified at the expression of any hope of realising a higher standard of comfort in this matter of housing than their most miserable palliation of the evil; because they cannot help feeling that the hope of Revolution must consciously or unconsciously underlie the hope of a somewhat higher standard, and that when this becomes obvious, as it soon must, the dominant class will shudder back from the whole subject, and bring to an end even the niggardly attempts of the 5 per cent. philanthropists. In case it should be said that I exaggerate the humility of the hopes of these latter good people, I refer to a letter written by the most practical of them, Miss Octavia Hill, to the *Pall Mall Gazette* in the past spring, in which she actually allows herself to say that after all it is not so bad as one might think for a whole family to live in one room; by a *room* of course meaning the ordinary 12ft. sq. hutch of an east end house.

Now while we may well feel too stern of mood when we

think of the life-long tortures of the "poor" to laugh even sar-
donically at such a limitation to the hopes of the philanthropist,
I wish our friends to accept my assertion that Miss Hill is a well
intentioned, disinterested and kindly person, for in that very fact
lies the force of her words as an indictment of our present
society; she, a good and eminently practical woman, with plenty
of experience as to the extent to which it is possible to move the
rich to help, and how far it is possible to use that help for the
benefit of the "poor," is forced to reduce her standard down to
this point, lest the spectre of *confiscation* should rise to bar the way
against her.

That she is quite right to dread that spectre the behaviour of
the present hole-and-corner Royal Commission has doubtless
already told her; but we will leave her household paradise of one
room for a while, nor will we much concern ourselves with the
standard of decent housing held out by those huge masses of
brick and mortar, which are rising up in various parts of the town
to compete for the workman's scanty shillings against the close-
ness, squalor and huddled make-shift of the ordinary landlord;
bare, sunless, and grim bastilles, are these and look like embodied
night-mares of the hopeless thrift of the wage-slave; we will leave
them also, and try to give our *masters* the philanthropists some
idea of what we consider decent housing for the working classes.

It might be advisable, granting the existence of huge towns
for the present, that the houses for workers should be built in
tall blocks, in what might be called vertical streets, but that need
not prevent ample room in each lodging, so as to include such
comforts of space, air, and privacy as every moderately-living
middle-class family considers itself entitled to; also it *must* not
prevent the lodgings having their due share of pure air and
sunlight, necessaries of life which the builders of the above
mentioned bastilles do not seem to have thought of at all. This
gathering of many small house into a big tall one would give
opportunity for what is also necessary to decent life, that is

garden space round each block. This space once obtained, it would be a small matter to make the gardens far more beautiful, as they would be certainly far more cheerful, than the square gardens of the aristocratic quarters of the town now are; it would be natural to have cloisters or covered walking or playing places in them, besides such cheap ornaments as fountains and conduits. Inside the houses, beside such obvious conveniences as common laundries and kitchens, a very little arrangement would give the dwellers in them ample and airy public rooms in addition to their private ones; the top story (*sic*) of each block might well be utilised for such purposes, the great hall for dining in, and for social gathering, being the chief feature of it.

Of course it is understood that such public rooms would not interfere with the ordinary private life of each family or individual; they would be there for use, if any one wished to use them, as they quite certainly would, for the avoidance of waste and the fostering of reasonable pleasure. I cannot be expected to forego the hint that these houses will be in no degree bare or prison-like: many cottages of the 10s. per week agricultural labourer that I have seen avoid that fault at any rate, and I can't see how it is possible that the city craftsman, with his habit of work and almost instinctive general capacity, should err on that side, if he had any starting point of hope given him, and proper leisure from mere bread-winning toil. I am quite sure that due co-operation among the men of diverse crafts who would inhabit these houses would make them not merely comfortable and pretty, but beautiful even.

The possession of space and pure air, with the determination not to live in the midst of ugliness, which relief from anxiety and overwork would give our mechanics, who are ingenious and ready-witted still in spite of their slavery, would supply the stimulus for such town-houses being made proper dwellings for human beings, even in the transition period between the anarchy of to-day and the social order which is to come. A fair portion of the earth's surface, due leisure for the exercise of thought, ingenuity, and fancy; that is all we ask for making our dwellings healthful, pleasant, and beautiful. Yes, that is *all!* Ah, fellow-workers, it is no use asking our *masters* for these necessaries: they *cannot* give them to us; there they sit in the Royal Commission asking—the Lord knows who—whether we have got these good things now, and whether if we have not got them we want them!

Understand this clearly, as long as labour, that is the lives of strong and deft men; is a *commodity* which can only be bought when it yields a profit to the non-worker, we cannot be allowed to use the earth to *live on* like men; it is all wanted for us to *work on* like machines: and just as much of the produce of our work will be given to us as will keep the *machines* going.

Workmen of England, you are just now agitating or being agitated for the purpose of obtaining the suffrage for some of you who have not had it before; this you do, I am ready to believe, with the ultimate intention of getting the suffrage for all adult persons. This agitation may be worth the trouble if you make up your minds that when you get the suffrage you will vote that you shall be machines no longer, and see that your vote is carried out. For what is a machine? Is it not a force of labour which has no control over its labour, but must be set a-going by a master?

Fellow-workers, what you have to do to determine that you will be men, not machines, and will have full control as a body over your own labour, that you will organise it for the good of each of you and all of you. If you determine on this whatever it may cost, and it is worth any cost, you will obtain it, with the suffrage or without it: if you do not so determine, you may get the suffrage, but it will be given to machines; and then as to this matter of housing you can at the best only be housed as careful masters house their machines. Alas! I fear that many of you will be housed as *careless* masters house them.

THE REVIVAL OF ARCHITECTURE

1888

Among cultivated people at present there is a good deal of interest felt or affected in the ornamental arts and their prospects. Since all these arts are dependent on the master-art of architecture almost for their existence, and cannot be in a healthy condition if it is sick, it may be worth while to consider what is the condition of architecture in this country; whether or now we have a living style which can lay claim to a dignity or beauty of its own, or whether our real style is merely a habit of giving certain forms not worth noticing to an all-pervading ugliness and meanness.

In the first place, then, it must be admitted on all sides that there has been in this century something like a revival of architecture; the question follows whether that revival indicates a genuine growth of real vitality which is developing into something else, or whether it merely points to a passing wave of fashion, which, when passed, will leave nothing enduring behind it. I can think of no better way of attempting a solution of this question than the giving a brief sketch of the history of this revival as far as I have noted it. The revival of the art of architecture in Great Britain may be said to have been a natural consequence of the rise of the romantic school in literature, although it lagged some way behind it, and naturally so, since the art of building has to deal with the prosaic incidents of every day life, and is limited by the material exigencies of its existence. Up to a period long after the death of Shelley and Keats and Scott, architecture could do nothing but produce on the one hand pedantic imitations of classical architecture of the most revolting ugliness, and ridiculous travesties of Gothic buildings, not quite so ugly, but meaner and sillier; and, on the other hand, the utilitarian brick box with a slate lid which the Anglo-Saxon generally in modern times considers as a good sensible house with no nonsense about it.

The first symptoms of change in this respect were brought about by the Anglo-Catholic movement, which must itself be considered as part of the romantic movement in literature, and was supported by many who had no special theological tendencies, as a protest against the historical position and stupid isolation of Protestantism. Under this influence there arose a genuine study of mediaeval architecture, and it was slowly discovered that it was not, as was thought in the days of Scott, a mere accidental jumble of picturesqueness consecrated by ruin and the lapse of time, but a logical and organic style evolved as a matter of necessity from the ancient styles of the classical peoples, and advancing step by step with the changes in the social life of barbarism and feudalism and civilization. Of course it took long to complete this discovery, nor as a matter of fact is it admitted in practice by many of the artists and architects of to-day, though the best of them feel, instinctively perhaps, the influence of the new school of historians, of whom the late John Richard Green and Professor Freeman may be cited as examples, and who have long been familiar with it.[1]

One unfortunate consequence the study of mediaeval art brought with it, owing indeed to the want of the admission of its historical evolution just mentioned. When the architects of this country had learned something about the building and ornament of the Middle Ages, and by dint of sympathetic study had more or less grasped the principles on which the design of that period was founded, they had a glimmer of an idea that those principles

belonged to the aesthetics of all art in all countries, and were
capable of endless development; they saw dimly that Gothic art
has been a living organism, but though they knew that it has
perished, and that its place had been taken by something else,
they did not know why it had perished, and thought it could be
artificially replanted in a society totally different from that which
gave birth to it. The result of this half-knowledge led them to
believe that they had nothing to do but to design on paper
according to the principles the existence of which they had
divined in Gothic architecture, and that the buildings so
designed, when carried out under their superintendence, would
be true examples of the ancient style, made alive by those
undying principles of the art. On this assumption it was natural
that they should attempt with confidence to remedy the injuries
and degradations which the ignorance, brutality, and vulgarity of
the post-Gothic periods had brought on those priceless treasures
of art and history, the buildings yet left to us from the Middle
Ages. Hence arose the fatal practice of "restoration," which in a
period of forty years has done more damage to our ancient buildings than the preceding three centuries of revolutionary violence,
sordid greed (utilitarianism so called), and pedantic contempt.
This side of the subject I have no space to dwell on further here.
I can only say that if my subject could be looked on from no
other point of view than the relation of modern architecture to
the preservation of these relics of the past, it would be most
important to face the facts of the present condition of the art
amongst us, lest a mere delusion as to our position should lead
us to throw away these treasures which once lost can never be
recovered. No doubt, on the other hand, this same half-knowledge gave the new school of architects courage to carry on their
work with much spirit, and as a result we have considerable
number of buildings throughout the country which do great
credit to the learning and talent of their designers, and some
of them even show signs of genius struggling through the

difficulties which beset an architect attempting to produce beauty in the midst of the most degrading utilitarianism.

In the early period of this Gothic revival the buildings thus produced were mostly ecclesiastical. The public were easily persuaded that the buildings destined for the use of the Anglican Church, which was obviously in part a survival from the Church of the Middle Ages, should be of the style which obtained in the period to which the greater part of its buildings belonged; and indeed it used to be customary to use the word "ecclesiastical" as a synonym for mediaeval architecture. Of course this absurdity was exploded among the architects at a very early stage of the revival, although it lingered long and perhaps still lingers amongst the general public. It was soon seen by those who studied the arts of the Middle Ages that there was no difference in style between the domestic and civil and the ecclesiastical architecture of that period, and the full appreciation of this fact marks the second stage in the "Gothic Revival."

Then came another advance: those who sympathized with that great period of the development of the human race, the Middle Ages, especially such of them as had the gift of the historical sense which may be said to be a special gift of the nineteenth century, and a kind of compensation for the ugliness which surrounds our lives at present: these men now began not only to understand that the mediaeval art was no mere piece of reactionary official ecclesiasticism or the expression of an extinct theology, but a popular, living, and progressive art—and that progressive art had died with it; they came to recognize that the art of the sixteenth and seventeenth centuries drew what vigour and beauty it had from the impulse of the period that preceded it, and that when that died out about the middle of the seventeenth century nothing was left but a *caput mortuum* of inanity and pedantry, which demanded perhaps a period of stern utilitarianism to form, as it were, the fallow of the arts before the new seed could be sown.

Both as regards art and history this was an important discovery. Undismayed by their position of isolation from the life of the present, the leaders of this fresh renaissance set themselves to the stupendous task of taking up the link of historical art where the pedants of the older so-called renaissance had dropped it, and tried to prove that the mediaeval style was capable of new life and fresh development, and that it could adapt itself to the needs of the nineteenth century. On the surface this hope of theirs seemed justified by the marvellous elasticity which the style showed in the period of its real life. Nothing was too great or too little, too commonplace or too sublime for its inclusive embrace; no change dismayed it, no violence seriously checked it; in those older days it was a part of the life of man, the universal, indispensable expression of his joys and sorrows. Could it not be so again? we thought; had not the fallow of the arts lasted long enough? Were the rows of square brown brick boxes which Keats and Shelley had to look on, or the stuccoed villa which enshrined Tennyson's genius, to be the perpetual concomitant of such masters of verbal beauty; was no beauty but the beauty of words to be produced by man in our times; was the intelligence of the age to be for ever so preposterously lop-sided? We could see no reason for it, and accordingly our hope was strong; for though we had learned something of the art and history of the Middle Ages, we had not learned enough. It became the fashion amongst the hopeful artists of the time I am thinking of to say that in order to have beautiful surroundings there was no need to alter any of the conditions and manners of our epoch; that an easy chair, a piano, a steam-engine, a billiard-table, or a hall fit for the meeting of the House of Commons, had nothing essential in them which compelled us to make them ugly, and that if they had existed in the Middle Ages the people of the time would have made them beautiful. Which certainly had an element of truth in it, but was not all the truth. It was indeed true that the mediaeval instinct for beauty would have exercised itself on whatsoever fell to its lot to do, but it was also true that the life of the times did not put into the hands of the workman any object which was merely utilitarian, still less vulgar; whereas the life of modern times forces on him the production of many things which can be nothing but utilitarian, as for instance a steam-engine; and of many things in which vulgarity is innate and inevitable, as a gentlemen's club-house or the ceremonial of our modern bureaucratic monarchy. Anyhow, this period of fresh hope and partial insight produced many interesting buildings and other works of art, and afforded a pleasant time indeed to the hopeful but very small minority engaged in it, in spite of all vexations and disappointments. At last one man, who had done more than any one else to make this hopeful time possible, drew a line sternly through these hopes founded on imperfect knowledge. This man was John Ruskin. By a marvellous inspiration of genius (I can call it nothing else) he attained at one leap to a true conception of mediaeval art which years of minute study had not gained for others. In his chapter in "The Stones of Venice," entitled "On the Nature of Gothic, and the Function of the Workman therein," he showed us the gulf which lay between us and the Middle Ages. From that time all was changed; ignorance of the spirit of the Middle Ages was henceforth impossible, except to those who wilfully shut their eyes. The aims of the new revival of art grew to be infinitely greater than they had been in those who did not give up all aim, as I fear many did. From that time forth those who could not learn the new knowledge were doomed to become pedants, differing only in the externals of the art they practised or were interested in from the unhistorical big-wigs of the eighteenth century. Yet the essence of what Ruskin then taught us was simple enough, like all great discoveries. It was really nothing more recondite than this, that the art of any epoch must of necessity be the expression of its social life, and that the social life of the Middle Ages allowed the workman freedom of individual expression, which on the other hand our social life forbids him.

I do not say that the change in the Gothic revivalists produced by this discovery was sudden, but it was effective. It has gradually sunk deep into the intelligence of the art and literature of to-day, and has had a great deal to do with the sundering of the highest culture (if one must use that ugly word) into a peculiarly base form of cynicism on the one hand, and into practical and helpful altruism on the other. The course taken by the Gothic revival in architecture, which, as aforesaid, is the outward manifestation of the Romantic school generally, shows decided tokens of the growing consciousness of the essential difference between our society and that of the Middle Ages. When our architects and archaeologists first mastered, as they supposed, the practice and principles of Gothic art, and began the attempt to reintroduce it as a universal style, they came to the conclusion that they were bound to take it up at the period when it hung balanced between completion and the very first beginnings of degradation. The end of the thirteenth and beginning of the fourteenth century was the time they chose as that best fitted for the foundation of the Neo-Gothic style, which they hoped was destined to conquer the world; and in choosing this period on the verge of transition they showed remarkable insight and appreciation of the qualities of the style. It had by that time assimilated to itself whatever it could use of classical art, mingled with the various elements gathered from the barbaric ancient monarchies and the northern tribes, while for itself it had no consciousness of them, nor was in any way trammelled by them; it was flexible to a degree yet undreamed of in any previous style of architecture, and had no difficulties in dealing with any useful purpose, any material or climate; and with all this is was undeniably and frankly beautiful, cumbered by no rudeness, and degraded by no whim. The hand and the mind of man, one would think, can carry loveliness (a loveliness, too, that never cloys) no further than in the architectural works of that period, as for instance in the choir and transepts of Westminster Abbey before it had suffered from degradations of later days, which truly make one stand aghast at the pitch of perversity which men can reach at times. It must be remembered too, in estimating the judgment of the Neo-Gothic architects, that the half-century from 1280 to 1320 was the blossoming-time of architecture all over that part of the world which had held fast to historical continuity; and the East as well as the West produced its loveliest works of ornament and art at that period. This development, moreover, was synchronous with the highest point of the purely mediaeval organization of industry. By that time the Gild-merchants and Lineages of the free towns, which had grown aristocratic, exclusive, and divorced from actual labour, had had to yield to the craft-gilds, democratic bodies of actual workmen, which had now taken the position that they had long striven for, and were the masters of all industry. It was not the monasteries, as we used to be told, which were the hives of the art of the fourteenth century, but the free towns with their crafts organized for battle as well as craftsmanship; not the reactionary but the progressive part of the society of the time.

This central period therefore of the Gothic style which expressed the full development of the social system of the Middle Ages, was undoubtedly the fittest period to choose for the tree on which to graft the young plant of Neo-Gothic; and at the time of which I am now thinking every architect of promise would have repudiated with scorn the suggestion that he should use any later or impurer style for the works he had to carry out. Indeed there was a tendency, natural enough, to undervalue the qualities of the later forms of Gothic, a tendency which was often carried to grotesque extremes, and the semi-Gothic survivals of the late sixteenth and the seventeenth centuries were looked on with mere contempt, in theory at least. But as time past and the revivalists began to recognize, whether they would or no, the impossibility of bridging the gulf between the fourteenth and the nineteenth centuries; as in spite of their brilliant individual successes they found themselves compelled to admit that the Neo-Gothic graft refused to grow in the commercial air of the Victorian era; as they toiled conscientiously and wearily to reconcile the Podsnappery of modern London with the expression of the life of Simon de Montfort and Philip van Artevelde, they discovered that they had pitched their note too high, and must try again, or give up the game altogether. By that time they had thoroughly learned the merits of the later Gothic styles, and even of the style which in England at least (as in literature so in art) had retained some of the beauty and fitness of the palmy days of Gothic amidst the conceits, artificialities, and euphuism of the time of Elizabeth and James the First; nay, they began to overvalue the remains of the inferior styles, not through pedantry, but rather perhaps from sympathy with the course of history, and repulsion from the pessimism which narrows the period of high aspirations and pleasure in life to the standard of our own passing moods. In the main, however, they were moved in this direction by the hope of finding another standpoint for the new and living style which they still hoped to set on foot; the elasticity and adaptability of the style of the fifteenth century, of which every village church in England gives us examples, and the great mass of the work achieved by it, in domestic as well as church architecture, ready to hand for study, as well as the half-conscious feelings of its being nearer to our own times and expressing a gradually-growing complexity of society, captivated the revivalists with a fresh hope. The dream of beauty and romance of the fourteenth century was gone; might not the more work-a-day "Perpendicular" give us a chance for the housing of Mr. Podsnap's respectability and counting-house, and bosom-of-the-family, and Sunday worship, without too manifest an absurdity?

So the architects began on the fifteenth-century forms, and as by this time they had gained more and more knowledge of mediaeval aims and methods, they turned out better and better work; but still the new living style would not come. The Neo-Gothic in the fourteenth-century style was often a fair rendering of its original; the fifteenth-century rendering has been often really good, and not seldom has had an air of originality about it that makes one admire the capacity and delicate taste of its designers;[2] but nothing comes of it; it is all hung in the air, so to say. London has not begun to look like a fifteenth-century city, and no flavour of beauty or even of generous building has begun to make itself felt in the numberless houses built in the suburbs.

Meantime from the fifteenth century we have sunk by a natural process to imitating something later yet, something so much nearer our own time and our own manners and ways of life, that a success might have been expected to come out of this at least. The brick style in vogue in the time of William the Third and Queen Anne is surely not too sublime for general use; even Podsnap might acknowledge a certain amount of kinship with the knee-breeched, cocked-hatted bourgeois of that period; might not the graft of the new style begin to grow now, when we have abandoned the Gothic altogether, and taken to a style that belongs to the period of the workshop and division of labour, a period when all that was left of the craft-gilds was the corruption of them, the mere abuses of the close corporations and companies under whose restrictions of labour the commercial class chafed so sorely, and which they were on the point of sweeping away entirely?

Well, it is true that at first sight the Queen Anne development has seemed to conquer modern taste more or less; but in truth it is only the barest shadow of it which has done so. The turn that some of our vigorous young architects (they were young then) took towards this latest of all domestic styles can be accounted for without quarrelling with their good taste or good sense. In truth, with the best of them it was not the differentia of the Queen Anne style that was the attraction; all that is a mere bundle of preposterous whims; it was the fact that in the style

there was yet left some feeling of the Gothic, at least in places or
under circumstances where the buildings were remote from the
progressive side of the eighteenth century. There I say some of
the Gothic feeling was left, joined to forms, such as sash
windows, yet possible to be used in our own times. The architects in search of a style might well say: "We have been driven
from ditch to ditch; cannot we yet make a stand? The un-
approachable grace and loveliness of the fourteenth century is
hull down behind us, the fifteenth-century work is too delicate
and too rich for the commonplace of to-day; let us be humble,
and begin once more with the style of well-constructed, fairly
proportioned brick houses which stand London smoke well, and
look snug and comfortable at some village end, or amidst the
green trees of a squire's park. Besides, our needs as architects are
not great; we don't want to build churches any more; the nobility
have their palaces in town and country already" (I wish them joy
of some of them!); "the working man cannot afford to live in
anything that an architect could design; moderate-sized rabbit-
warrens for rich middle-class men, and small ditto for the
hanger-on groups to which we belong, is all we have to think of.
Perhaps something of a style might arise amongst us from these
lowly beginnings, though indeed we have come down a weary
long way from Pugin's 'Contrasts.' We agree with him still, but
we are driven to admire and imitate some of the very things he
cursed, with our enthusiastic approbation." Well, a goodish many
houses of this sort have been built, to the great comfort of the
dwellers in them, I am sure; but the new style is so far from
getting under way, that while on the other hand the ordinary
builder is covering England with abortions which make us regret
the brick box and slate lid of fifty years ago, the cultivated classes
are rather inclined to return to the severity (that is to say, the
unmitigated expensive ugliness) of the last dregs of would-be
Palladian, as exemplified in the stone lumps of the Georgian
period. Indeed I have not heard that the "educated middle

classes" had any intention of holding a riotous meeting on the adjacent Trafalgar Square to protest against the carrying out of the designs for the new public offices which the Aedileship of Mr. Shaw-Lefevre[3] threatened us with. As to public buildings, Mr. Street's Law Courts [plate 6] are the last attempt we are likely to see of producing anything reasonable or beautiful for that use; the public has resigned itself to any mass of dulness and vulgarity that it may be convenient for a department to impose upon it, probably from a half-conscious impression that at all events it will be good enough for the work (so-called) which will be done in it.

In short we must answer the question with which this paper began by saying that the architectural revival though not a mere piece of artificial nonsense, is too limited in its scope, too much confined to an educated group, to be a vital growth capable of true development. The important fact in it is that it is founded on the sympathy for history and the art of historical generalization, which, as aforesaid, is a gift of our epoch, but unhappily a gift in which few as yet have a share. Among populations where this gift is absent, not even scattered attempts at beauty in architecture are now possible, and in such places generations may live and die, if society as at present constituted endures, without feeling any craving for beauty in their daily lives; and even under the most favourable circumstances there is no general impulse born out of necessity towards beauty, which impulse alone can produce a universal architectural style, that is to say, a habit of elevating and beautifying the houses, furniture, and other material surroundings of our life.

All we have that approaches architecture is the result of a quite self-conscious and very laborious eclecticism, and is avowedly imitative of the work of past times, of which we have gained a knowledge far surpassing that of any other period. Meanwhile whatever is done without conscious effort, that is to say the work of the true style of the epoch, is an offence to the sense of beauty and fitness, and is admitted to be so by all men who have any perception of beauty of form. It is no longer passively but actively ugly, since it has added to the dreary utilitarianism of the days of Dr. Johnson a vulgarity which is the special invention of the Victorian era. The genuine style of that era is exemplified in the jerry-built houses of our suburbs, the stuccoed marine-parades of our watering-places, the flaunting corner public-houses of every town in Great Britain, the raw-boned hideousness of the houses that mar the glorious scenery of the Queen's Park at Edinburgh. These form our true Victorian architecture. Such works as Mr. Bodley's excellent new buildings at Magdalen College [plate 4], Mr. Norman Shaw's elegantly fantastic Queen Anne houses at Chelsea [plate 5], or Mr. Robson's simple but striking London board-schools [plate 3], are mere eccentricities with which the public in general has no part or lot.

This is stark pessimism, my readers may say. Far from it. The enthusiasm of the Gothic revivalists died out when they were confronted by the fact that they form part of a society which will not and cannot have a living style, because it is an economical necessity for its existence that the ordinary everyday work of its population shall be mechanical drudgery; and because it is the harmony of the ordinary everyday work of the population which produces Gothic, that is, living architectural art, and mechanical drudgery cannot be harmonized into art. The hope of our ignorance has passed away, but it has given place to the hope born of fresh knowledge. History taught us the evolution of architecture, it is now teaching us the evolution of society; and it is clear to us, and even to many who refuse to acknowledge it, that the society which is developing out of ours will not need or endure mechanical drudgery as the lot of the general population; that the new society will not be hag-ridden as we are by the necessity for producing ever more and more market-wares for a profit, whether any one needs them or not; that it will produce to live, and not live to produce, as we do. Under such conditions architecture, as a part of the life of people in general, will again become possible, and I believe that when it is possible, it will have a real new birth, and add so much to the pleasure of life that we shall wonder how people were ever able to live without it. Meantime we are waiting for that new development of society, some of us in cowardly inaction, some of us amidst hopeful work towards the change; but at least we are all waiting for what must be the work, not of the leisure and taste of a few scholars, authors, and artists, but of the necessities and aspirations of the workmen throughout the civilized world.

Notes

1   *Short History of the English People* (1874) by John Richard Green (1837–83) treated history as a social rather than a political process. Edward Augustus Freeman (1823–92) was Regius Professor of Modern History at Oxford from 1884. In the mid 1870s he, like Morris, came out strongly against British Imperial interests.

2   See R. Dixon and S. Muthesius, *Victorian Architecture* (London: Thames and Hudson, 1978), pp. 222-8.

3   George John Shaw Lefevre (1831–1924) was appointed First Commissioner of Works following Gladstone's victory in 1880. A Liberal with radical leanings, he was a strong supporter of landscape conservation and improved public access to commons, footpaths and historic sites. An account of the architectural improvements carried out in London during his ministry is to be found in *The Nineteenth Century*, 19 (November 1888), pp. 703-18.

UGLY LONDON

1889

Ouida's article on the ugliness of London does, as you suggest, call for remarks from those who care at all for the real pleasure of life for themselves and others. But the subject is so wide that to begin with I had better limit it; for, as has been often said, London is not a town but a country covered with houses. Now, the London which presents itself to Ouida is not the London of the matchmakers and dock labourers in the East, or of the brickmakers and gas-workers of the west; she is not thinking of the slums beyond Bethnal-green, or those of Fulham and Latimer road, but of the shops and dwellings of the bourgeoisie, middle and upper (for England has no aristocracy). Of this well-to-do London, therefore, I will say a few words.

And first that her criticism of it is quite undeniable. I admit that it is not fair to compare bourgeois London with Venice, which is still a mediaeval city; or with Florence, which, though for years past now completely modernized, contains so many glorious monuments of the times of art. The proper city to compare London with is Paris, which is now entirely modern, and like London is not a mere makeshift accessory to a set of workshops, an encampment of capitalists and their machines, as are Manchester, Glasgow, and Birmingham, but a centre, political, social and intellectual, of a great system. Well, there are, I should think, few Londoners who do not feel exhilarated and happy with the change from London to Paris, who are not forced to admit that they have left something which is not pleasant and come to something which is. And yet please to note that, except for a few monuments of art, the buildings in Paris are quite without beauty, and are generally actively ugly. Paris is no longer a beautiful city, but it is delightful compared with London. You can stroll with pleasure in Paris; in London you cannot, unless you are a philosopher or a fool; you can only go from one piece of business to another.

There is, indeed, as Ouida says, something soul-deadening and discouraging in the ugliness of London; other ugly cities may be rougher and more savage in their brutality, but none are so desperately shabby, so irredeemably vulgar as London. It is difficult to express in words the feeling with which this "cockney nightmare" burdens me; "discouraging" is still the best word I can find. Or may I call in an analogy drawn from another sense than that of sight? There are certainly smells which are more depressing and deadly to pleasure than those which are frankly the nastiest: the refuse of gasworks, the brickfields in the calm summer evening, the faint, sweet smell of a suspicious drain, the London wood pavement at two o'clock on a hot, close summer morning—these kinds of smells are more lowering than the kind of stench that drives one to write furiously to the district surveyor. And the quality of London ugliness is just of this heart sickening kind.

Well, I find that I can do little more than endorse Ouida's criticism on bourgeois London. As to the remedies for this shabby misery, I will suggest two or three things which might be done, but which I cannot venture to call "remedies." First a negative step. In case it should be possible to improve London streets architecturally, it would be well to abolish the Metropolitan Building Act[1] which, passed at a time when we had reached bottom in architectural degradation allows all sorts of shabby abortions to be set up, while it forces architects to forego many pieces of inventiveness and picturesqueness, or to attempt "squaring" the surveyor. For the rest, by all means as many trees in the streets as we can get; and, by the way, they should not be pruned like pear-trees in an orchard house, as the custom now is. They are almost all American planes, and whatever beauty can be got out of that tree is to be had by allowing it to grow freely; besides, the more they spread, the more they will hide the houses.

Again, bourgeois London would be made much pleasanter by taking away all the railings of the square gardens and throwing them open to the public. What grass was left in them should not be walked upon, but basketed or coped in, as is done in Paris. This would be no loss, as London trodden grass is a very depressing growth, and fine trees rising out of the pavement have a decidedly noble look.

You see these are feeble palliatives—attempts, that is, to make Hell happy, instead of a resolution to get rid of it; and yet the last of them is clearly impossible under the present state of things. In truth, the only point in which I seem to differ from Ouida is that whereas she says it would be easy to make bourgeois London joyous, I say it would not only be not easy, but impossible. It is unreasonable to expect it to be otherwise. Rich London is the creature of slum-London, of poor London; and though I do not say that the London slums are worse than those of other big cities, yet they together with the rich quarters make up the monstrosity we call London, which is at once the centre and the token of that slavery of commercialism which has taken the place of the slaveries of the past; and it is fitting that those who profit (?) by this slavery should have its results brought home to them most obviously in its headquarters. The sickening hideousness of London, the metropolis of the nation, which has worked out the sum of commercialism most completely, seems to me a mark of disgrace branded on our wire-drawn refinement to show that it is based on the worst kind of theft—legal stealing from the poor.

Note

1   There was, in fact, no single 'Building Act' until the consolidating one of 1894. Morris was referring to a series of acts and bye-laws administered by local authorities. For a discussion of the relevant legislation see C.C. Knowles and P.H. Pitt, *The History of Building Regulation in London 1189–1972* (London: The Architectural Press, 1972), pp. 75-85.

GOTHIC ARCHITECTURE

1889

By the word Architecture is, I suppose, commonly under-stood the art of ornamental building, and in this sense I shall often have to use it here. Yet I would not like you to think of its productions merely as well constructed and well proportioned buildings, each one of which is handed over by the architect to other artists to finish, after his designs have been carried out (as we say) by a number of mechanical workers, who are not artists. A true architectural work rather is a building duly provided with all necessary furniture, decorated with all due ornament, according to the use, quality, and dignity of the building, from mere mouldings or abstract lines, to the great epical works of sculpture and painting, which, except as decora-tions of the nobler form of such buildings, cannot be produced at all. So looked on, a work of architecture is a harmonious co-operative work of art, inclusive of all the serious arts, all those which are not engaged in the production of mere toys, or of ephemeral prettinesses.

Now, these works of art are man's expression of the value of life, and also the production of them makes his life of value: and since they can only be produced by the general good-will and help of the public, their continuous production, or the existence of the true Art of Architecture, betokens a society which, what-ever elements of change it may bear within it, may be called stable, since it is founded on the happy exercise of the energies of the most useful part of its population.

What the absence of this Art of Architecture may betoken in the long run it is not easy for us to say: because that lack belongs only to these later times of the world's history, which as yet we cannot fairly see, because they are too near to us; but clearly in the present it indicates a transference of the interest of civilised men from the development of the human and intellectual energies of the race to the development of its mechanical energies. If this tendency is to go along the logical road of development, it must be said that it will destroy the arts of design and all that is analogous to them in literature; but the logical outcome of obvious tendencies is often thwarted by the historical development; that is, by what I can call by no better name than the collective will of mankind; and unless my hopes deceive me, I should say that this process has already begun, that there is a revolt on foot against the utilitarianism which threatens to destroy the Arts; and that it is deeper rooted than a mere passing fashion. For myself I do not indeed believe that this revolt can effect much, so long as the present state of society lasts; but as I am sure that great changes which will bring about a new state of society are rapidly advancing upon us, I think it a matter of much importance that these two revolts should join hands, or at least should learn to understand one another. If the New society when it comes (itself the result of the ceaseless evolution of countless years of tradition) should find the world cut off from all tradition of art, all aspiration towards the beauty which man has proved that he can create, much time will be lost in running hither and thither after the new thread of art; many lives will be barren of a manly pleasure which the world can ill afford to lose even for a short time ...

Now, that Harmonious Architectural unit, inclusive of the arts in general, is no mere dream. I have said that it is only in these later times that it has become extinct: until the rise of modern society, no Civilisation, no Barbarism has been without it in some form; but it reached its fullest development in the Middle Ages, an epoch really more remote from our modern habits of life and thought than the older civilisations were, though an important part of its life was carried on in our own country by men of our own blood. Nevertheless, remote as those times are from ours, if we are ever to have architecture at all, we must take up the thread of tradition there and nowhere else, because that Gothic Architecture is the most completely organic form of the Art, which the world has seen; the break in the thread of tradition could only occur there: all the former developments tended thitherward, and to ignore this fact and attempt to catch up the thread before that point was reached, would be a mere piece of artificiality, betokening, not new birth, but a corruption into mere whim of the ancient traditions.

In order to illustrate this position of mine, I must ask you to allow me to run very briefly over the historical sequence of events which led to Gothic Architecture and its fall, and to pardon me for stating familiar and elementary facts which are necessary for my purpose ...

We may divide the history of the Art of Architecture into two periods, the Ancient and the Medieval: the Ancient again may be divided into two styles, the barbarian (in the Greek sense) and the classical. We have, then, three great styles to consider: The Barbarian, the Classical, and the Medieval. The two former, however, were partly synchronous, and at least overlapped somewhat. When the curtain of the stage of definite history first draws up, we find the small exclusive circle of the highest civilisation, which was dominated by Hellenic thought and science, fitted with a very distinctive and orderly architectural style. That style appears to us to be, within its limits, one of extreme refinement, and perhaps seemed so to those who originally practised it. Moreover, it is ornamented with figure-sculpture far advanced towards perfection even at an early period of its existence, and swiftly growing in technical excellence; yet for all that, it is, after all, a part of the general style of architecture of the Barbarian world, and only outgoes it in the excellence of its figure-sculpture and its refinement. The bones of it, its merely architectural part, are little changed from the Barbarian or primal building, which is a mere piling or jointing together of material, giving one no sense of growth in the building itself and no sense of the possibility of growth in the style.

The one Greek form of building with which we are really familiar, the columnar temple, though always built with blocks of stone, is clearly a deduction from the wooden god's-house or shrine, which was a necessary part of the equipment of the not very remote ancestors of the Periclean Greeks; nor had this god's-house changed so much as the city had changed from the Tribe, or the Worship of the City (the true religion of the Greeks) from the Worship of the Ancestors of the Tribe. In fact, rigid conservatism of form is an essential part of Greek architecture as we know it. From this conservatism of form there resulted a jostling between the building and its higher ornament. In early days, indeed, when some healthy barbarism yet clung to the sculpture, the discrepancy is not felt; but as increasing civilisation demands from the sculptors more naturalism and less restraint, it becomes more and more obvious, and more and more painful; till at last it becomes clear that sculpture has ceased to be a part of architecture and has become an extraneous art bound to the building by habit or superstition. The form of the ornamental building of the Greeks, then, was very limited, had no capacity in it for development, and tended to divorce from its higher or epical ornament. What is to be said about the spirit of it which ruled that form? This I think; that the narrow superstition of the form of the Greek temple was not a matter of accident, but was the due expression of the exclusiveness and aristocratic arrogance of the ancient Greek mind, a natural result of which was a demand for pedantic perfection in all the parts and details of a building; so that the inferior parts of the ornament are so slavishly subordinated to the superior, that no invention or individuality is possible in them, whence comes a kind of bareness and blankness, a rejection in short of all romance, which does not indeed destroy their interest as relics of past history, but which puts the style of them aside as any possible foundation for the style of the future architecture of the world ...

But long before classical art reached the last depths of that degradation, it had brought to birth another style of architecture, the Roman style, which to start with was differentiated from the Greek by having the habitual use of the arch forced upon it. To my mind, organic Architecture, Architecture which must necessarily grow, dates from the habitual use of the arch, which, taking into consideration its combined utility and beauty, must be pronounced to be the greatest invention of the human race. Until the time when man not only had invented the arch, but had gathered boldness to use it habitually, architecture was necessarily so limited, that strong growth was impossible to it. It was quite natural that a people should crystallize the first convenient form of building they might happen upon, or, like the Greeks, accept a traditional form without aspiration towards anything more complex or interesting. Till the arch came into use, building men were the slaves of conditions of climate, materials, kind of labour available, and so forth. But once furnished with the arch, man has conquered Nature in the matter of building; he can defy the rigours of all climates under which men can live with fair comfort: splendid materials are not necessary to him; he can attain a good result from shabby and scrappy materials. When he wants size and span he does not need a horde of war-captured slaves to work for him; the free citizens (if there be any such) can do all that is needed without grinding their lives out before their time. The arch can do all that architecture needs, and in turn from the time when the arch comes into habitual use, the main artistic business of architecture is the decoration of the arch; the only satisfactory style is that which never disguises its office, but adorns and glorifies it. This the Roman architecture, the first style that used the arch, did not do. It used the arch frankly and simply indeed, in one part of its work, but did not adorn it; this part of the Roman building must, however, be called engineering rather than architecture, though its massive and simple dignity is a wonderful contrast to the horrible and restless nightmare of modern engineering. In the other side of its work, the ornamental side, Roman building used the arch and adorned it, but disguised its office, and pretended that the structure of its buildings was still that of the lintel, and that the arch bore no weight worth speaking of ... It was in the height of the tax-gathering period of the Roman Peace, in the last days of Diocletian (died 313) in the palace of Spalato which he built himself to rest in after he was satiated with rule, that the rebel, Change first showed in Roman art, and that the builders admitted that their false lintel was false, and that the arch could do without it.

This was the first obscure beginning of Gothic or organic Architecture; henceforth till the beginning of the modern epoch all is growth uninterrupted, however slow ...

The first expression of this freedom is called Byzantine Art, and there is nothing to object to in the name. For centuries Byzantium was the centre of it, and its first great work in that city (the Church of the Holy Wisdom, built by Justinian in the year 540) remains its greatest work. The style leaps into sudden completeness in this most lovely building: for there are few works extant of much importance of earlier days. As to its origin, of course buildings were raised all through the sickness of classical art, and traditional forms and ways of work were still in use, and these traditions, which by this time included the forms of Roman building, were now in the hands of the Greeks. This Romano-Greek building in Greek hands met with traditions drawn from many sources. In Syria, the borderland of so many races and customs, the East mingled with the West, and Byzantine art was born. Its characteristics are simplicity of structure and outline of mass; amazing delicacy of ornament combined with abhorrence of vagueness: it is bright and clear in colour, pure in line, hating barrenness as much as vagueness; redundant, but not florid, the very opposite of Roman architecture in spirit, though it took so many of its forms and revivified them. Nothing more beautiful than its best works has ever been produced by man, but in spite of its stately loveliness & quietude, it was the mother of fierce vigour in the days to come, for from its first days in St. Sophia, Gothic architecture has still one thousand years of life before it. East and West it overran the world wherever men built with history behind them ...

Here on the verge of a new change, a change of form important enough (though not a change of essence), we may pause to consider once more what its essential qualities were. It was the first style since the invention of the arch that did due honour to it, and instead of concealing it decorated it in a logical manner. This was much; but the complete freedom that it had won, which indeed was the source of its ingenuousness, was more. It had shaken off the fetters of Greek superstition and aristocracy, and Roman pedantry, and though it must needs have had laws to be a style at all, it followed them of free will, and yet unconsciously. The cant of the beauty of simplicity (i.e., bareness and barrenness) did not afflict it; it was not ashamed of redundancy of material, or super-abundance of ornament, any more than nature is. Slim elegance it could produce, or sturdy solidity, as its moods went. Material was not its master, but its servant: marble was not necessary to its beauty; stone would do, or brick, or timber. In default of carving it would set together cubes of glass or whatsoever was shining and fair-hued, and cover every portion of its interiors with a fairy coat of splendour ... Smoothness it loves, the utmost finish that the hand can give; but if material or skill fail, the rougher work shall so be wrought that it also shall please us with its inventive suggestion. For the iron rule of the classical period, the acknowledged slavery of every one but the great man, was gone, and freedom had taken its place ...

The full measure of this freedom Gothic Architecture did not gain until it was in the hands of the workmen of Europe, the gildsmen of the Free Cities, who on many a bloody field proved how dearly they valued their corporate life by the generous valour with which they risked their individual lives in its defence.

But from the first, the tendency was towards this freedom of hand and mind subordinated to the co-operative harmony which made the freedom possible. That is the spirit of Gothic Architecture ...

Certainly this change in form, when it came, was a startling one: the pointed-arched Gothic, when it had grown out of its brief and most beautiful transition, was a vigorous youth indeed. It carried combined strength and elegance almost as far as it could be carried: indeed, sometimes one might think it overdid the lightness of effect, as e.g., in the interior of Salisbury Cathedral. If some abbot or monk of the eleventh century could have been brought back to his rebuilt church of the thirteenth, he might almost have thought that some miracle had taken place: the huge cylindrical or square piers transformed into clusters of slim, elegant shafts; the narrow round-headed windows supplanted by tall wide lancets showing the germs of the elaborate traceries of the next century, and elegantly glazed with pattern and subject; the bold vault spanning the wide nave instead of the flat wooden ceiling of past days; the extreme richness of the mouldings with which every member is treated; the elegance and order of the floral sculpture, the grace and good drawing of the imagery: in short, a complete and logical style with no longer anything to apologise for, claiming homage from the intellect, as well as the imagination of men ...

This point of development was attained amidst a period of social conflict, the facts and tendencies of which, ignored by the historians of the eighteenth century, have been laid open to our view by our modern school of evolutionary historians. In the twelfth century the actual handicraftsmen found themselves at last face to face with the development of the earlier associations of freemen which were the survivals from the tribal society of Europe: in the teeth of these exclusive and aristocratic municipalities the handicraftsmen had associated themselves into guilds of craft, and were claiming their freedom from legal and arbitrary oppression, and a share in the government of the towns; by the end of the thirteenth century they had conquered the position everywhere and within the next fifty or sixty years the governors of the free towns were the delegates of the craftguilds, and all handicraft was included in their associations. This period of their triumph, marked amidst other events by the Battle of Courtray, where the chivalry of France turned their backs in flight before the Flemish weavers, was the period during which Gothic Architecture reached its zenith. It must be admitted, I think, that during this epoch, as far as the art of beautiful building is concerned, France and England were the architectural countries par excellence; but all over the intelligent world was spread this bright, glittering, joyous art, which had now reached its acme of elegance and beauty; and moreover in its furniture, of which I have spoken above, the excellence was shared in various measure betwixt the countries of Europe. And let me note in passing that the necessarily ordinary conception of a Gothic interior as being a colourless whitey-grey place dependent on nothing but the architectural forms, is about as far from the fact as the corresponding idea of a Greek temple standing in all the chastity of white marble. We must remember, on the contrary, that both buildings were clad, and that the noblest part of their raiment was their share of a great epic, a story appealing to the hearts and minds of men ...

For now Gothic Architecture had completed its furniture: Dante, Chaucer, Petrarch; the German Hero ballad-epics, the French Romances, the English Forest-ballads, that epic of revolt, as it has been called, the Icelandic Sagas, Froissart and the Chroniclers, represent its literature. Its painting embraces a host of names (of Italy and Flanders chiefly) the two great realists Giotto and Van Eyck at their head: but every village has its painter, its carvers, its actors even; every man who produces works of handicraft is an artist. The few pieces of household goods left of its wreckage are marvels of beauty; its woven cloths and embroideries are worthy of its loveliest building, its pictures and ornamented books would be enough in themselves to make a great period of art, so excellent they are in epic intention, in completeness of unerring decoration, and in marvellous skill of hand. In short, those masterpieces of noble building, those specimens of architecture, as we call them, the sight of which makes the holiday of our lives to-day, are the standard of the whole art of those times, and tell the story of all the completeness of art in the heyday of life, as well as that of the sad story which follows. For when anything human has arrived at quasi-completion there remains for it decay and death, in order that the new thing may be born from it; and this wonderful joyous art of the Middle Ages could by no means escape its fate.

In the middle of the fourteenth century Europe was scourged by that mysterious terror the Black Death (a terror similar to which perhaps waylays the modern world) and, along with it, the no less mysterious pests of Commercialism and Bureaucracy attacked us. This misfortune was the turning point of the Middle Ages; once again a great change was at hand.

The birth and growth of the coming change was marked by art with all fidelity. Gothic Architecture began to alter its character in the years that immediately followed on the Great Pest; it began to lose its exaltation of style and to suffer a diminution in the generous wealth of beauty which it gave us in its heyday. In some places, e.g., England, it grew more crabbed, and even sometimes more common-place; in others, as in France, it lost order, virility, and purity of line. But for a long time yet it was alive and vigorous, and showed even greater capacity than before for adapting itself to the needs of a developing society: nor did the change of style affect all its furniture injuriously; some of the subsidiary arts as e.g., Flemish tapestry and English wood-carving, rather gained than lost for many years ...

Society was preparing for a complete recasting of its element: the Medieval Society of Status was in process of transition into the modern Society of Contract. New classes were being formed to fit the new system of production which was at the bottom of this; political life began again with the new birth of bureaucracy;

and political, as distinguished from natural, nationalities were being hammered together for the use of that bureaucracy, which was itself a necessity to the new system. And withal a new religion was being fashioned to fit the new theory of life: in short, the Age of Commercialism was being born.

Now some of us think that all this was a source of misery and degradation to the world at the time, that it is still causing misery and degradation, and that as a system it is bound to give place to a better one. Yet we admit that it had a beneficent function to perform; that amidst all the ugliness and confusion which it brought with it, it was a necessary instrument for the development of freedom of thought and the capacities of man; for the subjugation of nature to his material needs. This Great Change, I say, was necessary and inevitable, and on this side, the side of commerce and commercial science and politics, was a genuine new birth. On this side it did not look backward but forward: there had been nothing like it in past history; it was founded on no pedantic model; necessity, not whim, was its crafts-master.

But, strange to say, to this living body of social, political, religious, scientific New Birth was bound the dead corpse of a past art. On every other side it bade men look forward to some change or other, were it good or bad: on the side of art, with the sternest pedagogic utterance, it bade men look backward across the days of the 'Fathers and famous men that begat them;' and in scorn of them, to an art that had been dead a thousand years before. Hitherto, from the very beginning the past was past, all of it that was not alive in the present, unconsciously to the men of the present. Henceforth the past was to be out present, and the blankness of its dead wall was to shut out the future from us ...

This used once to puzzle me in the presence of one of the so-called masterpieces of the New Birth, the revived classical style, such a building as St. Paul's in London, for example. I have found it difficult to put myself in the frame of mind which could accept such a work as a substitute for even the latest and worst Gothic building. Such taste seemed to me like the taste of a man who should prefer his lady-love bald. But now I know that it was not a matter of choice on the part of any one then alive who had an eye for beauty: if the change had been made on the grounds of beauty it would be wholly inexplicable; but it was not so. In the early days of the Renaissance there were artists possessed of the highest qualities; but those great men (whose greatness, mind you, was only in work not carried out by co-operation, painting, and sculpture for the most part) were really but the fruit of the blossoming-time, the Gothic period; as was abundantly proved by the succeeding periods of the Renaissance, which produced nothing but inanity and plausibility in all the arts. A few individual artists were great truly; but artists were no longer the masters of art, because the people had ceased to be artists; its masters were pedants. St. Peter's in Rome, St. Paul's in London, were not built to be beautiful, or to be beautiful and convenient. They were not built to be homes of the citizens in their moments of exaltation, their supreme grief or supreme hope, but to be proper, respectable, and therefore to show the due amount of cultivation and knowledge of the only peoples and times that in the minds of their ignorant builders were not ignorant barbarians. They were built to be the homes of a decent un-enthusiastic ecclesiasticism, of those whom we sometimes call Dons now-a-days. Beauty and romance were outside the aspirations of their builders. Nor could it have been otherwise in those days; for, once again, architectural beauty is the result of the harmonious and intelligence co-operation of the whole body of people engaged in producing the work of the workman; and by the time that the changeling New Birth was grown to be a vigorous imp, such workmen no longer existed. By that time Europe had begun to transform the great army of artists-craftsmen, who had produced the beauty of her cities, her churches, manor-houses and cottages, into an enormous stock of human machines, who had little chance of earning a bare livelihood if they lingered over their toil to think of what they were doing: who were not asked to think, paid to think, or allowed to think ...

But at present I am not going to say anything about direct remedies for the miseries of the New Birth; I can only tell you what you ought to do if you can. I want you to see that from the brief historic review of the progress of the Arts it results that to-day there is only one style of Architecture on which it is possible to found a true living art, which is free to adapt itself to the varying conditions of social life, climate, and so forth, and that that style is Gothic architecture. The greater part of what we now call architecture is but an imitation of an imitation of an imitation, the result of a tradition of dull respectability, or of foolish whims without root or growth in them.

Let us look at an instance of pedantic retrospection employed in the service of art. A Greek columnar temple when it was a real thing, was a kind of holy railing built round a shrine: these things the people of that day wanted, and they naturally took the form of a Greek Temple under the climate of Greece and given the mood of its people. But do we want those things? If so, I should like to know what for. And if we pretend we do and so force a Greek Temple on a modern city, we produce such a gross piece of ugly absurdity as you may see spanning the Lochs at Edinburgh. In these islands we want a roof and walls with windows cut in them; and these things a Greek Temple does not pretend to give us.

Will a Roman building allow us to have these necessaries? Well, only on the terms that we are to be ashamed of wall, roof and windows, and pretend that we haven't got either of them, but rather a whimsical attempt at the imitation of a Greek Temple.

Will a neo-classical building allow us these necessities? Pretty much on the same terms as the Roman one; except when it is rather more than half Gothic. It will force us to pretend that we have neither roof, walls, nor windows, nothing but an imitation of the Roman travesty of a Greek Temple.

Now a Gothic building has walls that it is not ashamed of; and in those walls you may cut windows wherever you please; and, if you please may decorate them to show that you are not ashamed of them; your windows, which you must have, become one of the great beauties of your house, and you have no longer to make a lesion in logic in order not to sit in pitchy darkness in your own house, as in the sham sham-Roman style: your window, I say, is no longer a concession to human weakness, an ugly necessity (generally ugly enough in all conscience) but a glory of the Art of Building. As for the roof in the sham style: unless the building is infected with Gothic common sense, you must pretend that you are living in a hot country which needs nothing but an awning, and that it never rains or snows in these islands. Whereas in a Gothic building the roof both within and without (especially within, as is most meet) is the crown of its beauties, the abiding place of its brain ...

Once for all, then, when the modern world finds that the eclecticism of the present is barren and fruitless, and that it needs and will have a style of architecture which, I must tell you once more, can only be as part of a change as wide and deep as that which destroyed Feudalism; when it has come to that conclusion, the style of architecture will have to be historic in the true sense; it will not be able to dispense with tradition; it cannot begin at least with doing something quite different from anything that has been done before; yet whatever the form of it may be, the spirit of it will be sympathy with the needs and aspirations of its own time, not simulation of needs and aspirations passed away. Thus it will remember the history of the past, make history in the present, and teach history in the future. As to the form of it, I see nothing for it but that the form, as well as the spirit, must be Gothic; an organic style cannot spring out of an eclectic one, but only from an organic one. In the future, therefore, our style of architecture must be Gothic Architecture ...

THE INFLUENCE OF BUILDING MATERIALS UPON ARCHITECTURE

1891

I am afraid after all that, though the subject is a very important one, yet there are so many of you present who must know all about it, that you will find what I have to say is little better than commonplace. Still, you know there are occasions and times when commonplaces have to be so to say hammered home, and even those who profess the noble art of architecture want a certain sort of moral support in that line; they know perfectly well what they ought to do, but very often they find themselves in such an awkward position that they cannot do it, owing no doubt to the stupidity of their clients, who after all are not so stupid as they might be, one may think, since they employ them. Nevertheless, their clients generally are not educated persons on the subject of architecture.

Now the subject of Material is clearly the foundation of architecture, and perhaps one would not go very far wrong if one defined architecture as the art of building suitably with suitable material. There are certainly many other things which are considered architectural, and yet not nearly so intimately and essentially a part of architecture, as a consideration of material. Also, it seems to me, there is one important thing to be considered with reference to material in architecture at the present time, when all people are seeking about for some sort of style. We know of course, and there is no use denying the fact, that we are in a period when style is a desideratum which everybody is seeking for, and which very few people find; and it seems to me that nothing is more likely to lead to a really living style than the consideration, first of all, as a *sine quâ non*, of the suitable use of material. In fact, I do not see how we are to have anything but perpetual imitation, eclectic imitation of this, that, and the other style in the past, unless we begin with considering what material lies about us, and how we are to use it, and the way to build it up in such a form as will really put us in the position of being architects, alive and practising to-day, and not merely architects handing over to a builder and to builder's men all the difficulties of the profession, and only keeping for ourselves that part of it which can be learnt in a mechanical and rule-of-thumb way.

Now I suppose, in considering the materials of a building, one ought to begin by considering the walls. I am not going to trouble myself very much about those materials which afford opportunities for the exercise of particular *finesse* in the way of architecture, but rather I shall refer to the more homely and everyday materials. I suppose one may fairly divide materials for the building of a wall into three sections; first stone, then timber, and lastly brick. In doing so, and in giving them that order, I distinctly myself mean to indicate the relative position of nobility between those three materials. Stone is definitely the most noble material, the most satisfactory material; wood is the next, and brick is a makeshift material.

Those of you who are architects I am quite sure know the difficulties that you find yourselves involved in when you have to build a stone building. You will find probably that your London builder is not by any means the best man to go to. The fact of the matter is, London builders have really ceased to understand the ground principles on which stone should be used. Now I think the consideration of stone buildings has this extreme importance about it, that when you fairly begin to consider how best to deal with stone as a material, you have begun then first to free yourself from the bonds of mere academic architecture. The academical architect, it seems to me, assumes as a matter of course that all buildings are built with ashlar on the face of them, and not only so, but that all stone buildings through and through are built with ashlar. That is the impression an academical building always gives me, that it is built of great cubes of stone as big as you can possibly get them; and very naturally, because it seems to be something like a canon in academical architecture that if you want a building bigger than the average buildings, you must increase every one of its members in order to get to that great size, and the net result is, that the whole of the members of that academic building are all one size, and as a rule they all look about the size of a Wesleyan Methodist meeting-house; that is, you lose all scale. It seems to me that the use of stone in a proper and considerate manner does in the first place lead to your being able to get a definite size and scale to a building. The building no longer looks, as so many renaissance buildings do, as if it might just as well be built of brick and plastered over with compo. You can see, in fact, the actual bones and structure. But it is something more than that; you can see in point of fact the life of it by studying the actual walls. This organic life of a building is so interesting, so beautiful even, that it is a distinct and definite pleasure to see a large blank wall without any ordinary architectural features, if it is really properly built and properly placed together. In point of fact this seems to me almost the beginning of architecture, that you can raise a wall which impresses you at once by its usefulness; its size, if it is big; its delicacy, if it is small; and in short by its actual life; that is the beginning of building altogether.

Now to go a little further into detail. The kind of building you want in different places is very different. There is a great deal of very beautiful building to be seen all about the country which is, in point of fact, built merely as a barn or a cart-shed is built; and I think it would be a great pity if we lost all that. We cannot build the whole of our buildings throughout the whole country in careful close-jointed ashlar, and I think it would be a great pity if we could; but the difference between the town and country, especially a big city, strikes me rather strongly in that respect. How many buildings one sees, big dignified buildings, gentlemen's country houses, standing in the middle of a park, or something of that kind, that are most inexpressibly dreary—to a great extent because they are not built in the ordinary fashion of the country-side in which they are raised, quite apart from any matter of architectural design. But in passing through the country one sees many examples of thoroughly good ordinary country buildings, built of the mere country materials, very often of the mere stones out of the fields; and it is a very great pleasure to see the skill with which these buildings are constructed. They are very often not pointed at all, but you cannot help noticing the skill with which the mason has picked out his longs and his shorts, and put the thing together with really something, you must say, like rhythm and measurement (his traditional skill that was), and with the best possible results. I cannot help thinking that on the whole London and the big towns are not places where stone building is usually desirable. There is only one stone, it seems to me, that looks tolerably well in London, and that is good Portland stone; and that looks well partly owing to the curious way in which the exposed parts of it get whistled by the wind, and the mouldings and hollows and all the rest of it get blackened, the very smoke even doing something probably for Portland stone in London. But you have plenty of examples of the disastrous effects of building with a great many stones that have been used in London. One unfortunate result of architectural research in the past: people were taught, when the Gothic revival first came in, that in old days in London they used to build with that rough stone out of Kent, rubble walls and stone dressings; so that there are heaps of Gothic churches of that date about the town, and it is almost a regular kind of sacramental word in the newspapers that criticize such matters: "built of

Kentish rag-stone with Bath stone dressings," and the result is very dismal on all hands. There is this wretched rag-stone, which was used at a time when there was no smoke in London, at a time when the inhabitants of London petitioned Edward the First against the introduction of pit-coal into London because it dirtied the houses; whereas nowadays no one seems inclined to petition against the introduction of smoke: and there it is; it blackens the rough rag-stone, and the sulphuric acid in the atmosphere utterly destroys the oolite limestone of Bath.

Now as for stone building, clearly in London one wants a smooth stone building, and if one cannot get a smooth stone building it seems to me that the next best thing is to have a building of good bricks; but I suppose the very words that I have mentioned, good bricks, are enough to raise up visions of all sorts of trouble and bother which architects here have in trying to get these good bricks; and I must say that in building with good bricks in London (if only you can get good bricks), I should like to see places built of good bricks, and entirely built of brick, with no attempt to add anything else to them. I think, as a rule, that is really all one wants in big towns. One has seen examples of exactly the contrary sort of work. Take for example the big municipal buildings in Manchester, built partly of brick and partly with freestone dressings, and so on. The freestone dressings are now getting a horrible dirty drab black, worse than a mere black, and the whole result is that whatever architecture there may be in the building is pretty much destroyed and obliterated by the dirt. If the building had been built entirely of brick it would have preserved its character; it would have got all darker together, and would have preserved it own outlines right away to the end, and, although you might have regretted the dustiness and dreariness of its blackening, yet still you would have had the real outline of the building, not confused with all this growing and obviously unavoidable dirt that it actually collected about it.

As to bricks, it is quite clear that we ought to make rather more efforts than are made to get the bricks better adapted to their work. I spoke just now about Broseley tiles. Just call to your memory the ordinary villages in the Midland counties of England, which I suppose were once pretty places. They are no longer pretty places at all. There are two reasons why they are ugly now; because the buildings, whatever they once were, have almost entirely given place to buildings built of the Midland county bricks, which are great big, stumpy, lumpy blocks of clay, a very bad colour as a rule; "excellent material" I believe builders would call them; and they are all roofed with these Staffordshire tiles, the worst peculiarity of which is that they never weather to a decent colour; a few months after they are put up they get a vile dirty sort of black colour, even in the country (it is not merely the smoke) and at that black colour they stick to the end of the chapter.

Well, I cannot go very much further than that, as far as the stone goes. To build country fashion in the country if possible would certainly be my advice, and in the town to do what you best can; to look the thing fairly and squarely in the face, and see what you can do to prevent your fine architecture from being made sheer nonsense.

The other material that I mentioned, the one that came second in my list of good materials, wood, is I suppose (I am speaking now of walls) a thing which cannot often be used nowadays. It seems to me to be mainly because you can no longer use wood as a material for a wall as frankly as it used to be used in mediaeval times, when good oak was almost a drug in the market. To build wooden houses with the framing of small dimensions seems to me one of the poorest things one can possibly do. You want, in point of fact, in order to build a satisfactory wooden house, to be able to indulge in the greatest possible generosity of material, to have no sparing whatever, or else your wooden house will look like nothing but a feeble attempt to imitate the results of the architecture of the past. So that, after all, in spite of my great liking for wood, for I think there is nothing more beautiful than a beautiful wooden house, I am afraid we must at present put the use of wood clean out of the question. We cannot build a house with wooden walls at present; the main material that walls must be built of nowadays is brick, and, therefore, again, I urge all architects to do the utmost they possibly can to get their bricks as well made and as well shaped as they can, that is to say, as long as possible and as narrow as possible, and to build them with wide joints of the very best mortar.

Now there is, by the way, another kindred material to brick, and that is the cast brick they call terra-cotta. I cannot abide it, I must say. I do not think I need treat it any further, and I will tell you why. It is used for nothing else except ornament, and I am rather inclined to think that of all things not wanted at the present day, and especially in London outside a house, the thing that is least wanted is ornament. That is to say, as long as there is a huge congeries of houses, as in London, the greater part of which are lamentably and hideously ugly, I think one ought to pitch one's note rather low, and try, if one can manage it, to get the houses and buildings to look solid and reasonable, and to impress people with their obvious adaptation to their uses; where they can be made big to make them big, and not to bother about ornament. Such ornament as there is, to keep it for the inside, where at all events it can be treated with delicacy, and you do not feel that you have something which after all, whatever value there is in it as ornament, will presently disappear, and you simply get something which is of no particular use, except for collecting dirt. You know perfectly well how that cast stuff is generally used; I noticed some as I came along just now, and I said to myself: After all, these things are not a bit like cast work, or moulded work at all; they look like a bad imitation of carved work. It has a fatal ease in the matter of ornamentation, which makes the material, it seems to me, decidedly bad for its purpose. I think it is very much better if you want to have brick ornament on a building to get cut and rubbed brick. From the point of view of ordinary practical and everyday use at the present time, I think it is hardly worth while in this country to talk about marble as a material; certainly not for the outside of a building. As a method of ornamentating wall surfaces on the inside marble is the most difficult material to use which it is possible to conceive. I do not know how it is, but unless it is used with the utmost skill, a skill which must, to be successful, be the result of many centuries of tradition—unless it is so used, the marble even in the inside does decidedly vulgarize the building, however beautiful it may be in itself.

Now we come to another point, which is the material of roofs; and this is, in a way, almost more important than the material of the walls of a building. First of all I have one thing to say, which is this. I am not tyrannically disposed, nor given to inciting the Government in its attempt to deal with the morals and feelings of its subjects; but I should be really rather glad, although I should not like to have a hand in it, if some Government were to forbid entirely the use of Welsh slates. If the Welsh slate quarries could be shut up by Act of Parliament, or by whatever may be stronger than an Act of Parliament, I think I myself should have a very good sleep, and a happy getting up in the morning afterwards. In point of fact, I think all architects ought to make up their minds to one thing, that the use of these Welsh slates does distinctly stamp a building as being merely the exhibition of the very depth of poverty. If you are so poor that you cannot help using Welsh slates, then use them, but in that case say to your client: I cannot under these circumstances degrade myself by attempting to make this building ornamental. It is not the work of an architect at all, it is simply a trumpery makeshift which is to be removed as soon as you have a little money; consequently I refuse to put any ornament on it; I will not have so much as a moulding of any kind. Here you have a shed (a very ugly shed, you ought to add); you know after all it is perfectly possible for a shed to be put up with no ornament at all which shall be a very beautiful thing, but I am afraid it is impossible to have architecture with these thin slates. Of course it is perfectly true that there are some beautiful buildings covered with these thin slates, but then I think one always looks at that as a mere blemish to be removed. One can conceive that the building, which is now roofed with slate, once was not roofed with slate, and one supposes it away, or else one would be so disgusted at the sight of it that one could hardly bear to look at the building at all. So that, I think, is the first thing to be thought of by all architects. How shall we possibly be able to manage not to roof our buildings however little there is to be spent upon it, with these miserable thin slates? Just consider the effect in places you have seen that comes of the use of a material that is better than ordinary slate. I have before my mind's eye now some of those big squares in Edinburgh for example. They are a very uninteresting set of buildings there, by no means exhilarating, yet the fact that they are most of them covered with something better than ordinary thin slate decidedly gives them a kind of pleasantness, and even a kind of dignity that they would not otherwise possess. You look out of your window in the morning from a portion of the city high up over the roofs; you look down upon them, and instead of giving you a pain in the stomach they really give you a certain kind of pleasure. There are a lot of these things all tumbled together, and they have a certain kind of interest in them, and the covering of them is after all tolerable. Of course it is possible, even in Wales, to roof things with something better than the ordinary slates that are used; because you may notice that in the little bits of cottages and farmhouses where there is no attempt at any sort of architecture, although the colour of the slates is not pleasant, yet they do not look quite so bad as they otherwise would, simply because the slates are a good thickness, and because they are chipped at the edges; being, I suppose, the waste of the quarries, and as a result they look pretty well.

I have often spoken to architects about this, and I find even architects who ought to know the merits of them are rather shy of using them. They give very excellent reasons, no doubt; the first, that if you have these heavy stone slates you must have timbers on the roof heavy. Very well, I should say in answer to that, If the roofs are not heavy enough to carry stone slates properly, they are not heavy enough to be roofs at all. You want that scantling of timber to make the roof really lasting, and this would enable it to carry stone slates perfectly easily. The other reasons, I suppose, for their not using them are constructional reasons, which perhaps resolve themselves into this; that it wants considerable care in selecting the slates, and that the quarrymen who sell the slates are naturally more anxious for the slates to be sold than for the roof to endure; and as a consequence it often turns out that they shove off on people bad wares. I cannot help thinking that with greater pains a great deal might be done in those countrysides where stone slates may be used. Take for example the city of Oxford, which is such a lamentable example of all kinds of architectural errors and mistakes, and I might almost say crimes. There, some time ago, when they were roofing the new buildings which I am very sorry to say they built there, like Exeter College Chapel,[1] they roofed them with stone slates. The stone slates, they found, year by year began to decay, and all went to the natural limestone dust. The result was they stripped the roofs and stuck green Westmoreland slates on. A very good thing is a green Westmoreland slate, it is said; and so it is in London on a red brick building, but on a grey stone building in Oxford it looks absolutely horrible. That is a very good example of the influence of material on architecture. Roof-coverings that do perfectly well in a certain style and in a certain place are most objectionable in another kind of style and in another place; and it seems to me perfectly clear that if all the colleges in Oxford had formed a committee to arrange about the roof-covering materials of their colleges, they might very easily have got almost into their pockets certain quarries in the neighbourhood or the neighbouring counties, and the result would have been that they might have got a continuous steady supply of the very best stone slates, which would have covered their buildings for hundreds of years, because the thing once started would have gone on. But they were so careless that they did not trouble themselves about it. It was also rather cheaper to roof the buildings with Westmoreland slates than with stone slates. University College, for example, saved the college the enormous sum of thirty pounds, I believe, in roofing the whole with the thin slates instead of the good ones. I must not dwell too long upon it, but I do earnestly direct your attention as architects to that matter of the roofing material, and especially where possible to get the people to raise some kind of demand for these stone slates. In our own immediate country we used to get slates from a village called Poulton, between Fairford and Cirencester. The Poulton slates were remarkably good at one time, but they are now going off, and all you can get now from Poulton is a sort of coagulated mud which is clearly not to be trusted as a roofing material, although it is nothing like as bad to look at as blue slates, or slates of that kind; and it is rather a hard slate, but it is not thoroughly satisfactory. I have not the slightest doubt that if two or three of the people about there, like the big landowner in my neighbourhood, who is a great patron of the arts and so on, would make an effort and demand these stone slates of a good bed, they would get them; because it would be worth people's while to open the quarries, and at a slight additional expense they might get them from countrysides which are not very remote; but what one sees going on there always is the perpetual worsening, especially in the roofing material of the buildings. It is rather remarkable that they still go on building stone walls for cart-sheds and all sorts of farm buildings, which, as far as the walls are concerned, are not so very bad, especially when they do not want them to be grand, and do not point them in a hideous manner; but the roofing is almost certain nowadays to be either thin blue slate or else that zinc-looking stuff. On the whole, I rather prefer that to blue slate, because you feel you can take it all off in a lump, and shove it on one side.

As to the use of thatch, I wish you could use it more often

than you do. It is used so little that there are now very few thatchers to be got. In fact it is the commonest thing, if you ask a person to do something, to cast lead for example, to hear: "I do not know how to do it; I cannot do it; my grandfather used to be able to do it." That is not at all an uncommon thing, and that is the road things are going. In point of fact, what has happened there is what happens in other ways, that the town has practically entirely invaded the country, and the countryside is now treated as a kind of back-yard of the counting-house. That is the fact of the matter, and everything is going down-hill as far as the exterior appearance is concerned. There is an agitation on foot just now about getting better houses for the agricultural labourers; but people will have to take great care that instead of getting better houses they do not get worse, which they are very likely to do at the rate they are going now. Some of you must have gone into those villages in Northamptonshire where there are some splendid examples of the old churches, and where the building material is very good; there is, for instance, that stone with an irony cast in it. In those villages you will see that a thing has happened which makes them the most miserable places you can see in the whole country. All the back gardens and yards have been built over with nasty little brick houses with blue slate roofs for the shoe-making trades, and so on. I cannot think that this improves the lodging of the country people, for the building is of the vilest possible description.

To sum up about this roofing material: it seems to me, you have really first of all lead for a good roof-covering; then you have stone slates; you have thatch, and you may have, with some trouble, a good country-made tile. This is an extremely difficult thing to get, mind you, because unfortunately the Broseley tiles are so largely used as an "excellent building material," that the country potters have got worse and worse, and the tiles they provide you with will hardly keep out the wet. That again is another thing that wants a sort of combination of people who have to do with building to insist, as far as they can, on having this material turned out as good as it possibly can be turned out, and to be always worrying and thinking about these things. Well, the tile of course is again a very serious affair, because over a large part of the country tiles, if you could get them good, are the most convenient roof-covering you can have. When they are good they are very pretty in their own countryside, but I must say I have seen them on what I should call a grey stone countryside, and there I think the tiles even when good are a kind of blight on the landscape. The beautiful greyness of the stone slate, the lovely tone of these old stone houses are better, especially for the home-like landscape you see in that part of the country, than anything that could take its place; it would be a misfortune if you had to use tiles rather than the old stone roofs. But in other parts of the country, tiles would do very well, especially if you have good tiles that weather properly, like some of the old tiles in Kent and Sussex.

But there is one last material, which I suppose there might be a difficulty about getting a man to accept, but which would be a very good material to use for roof-covering if it can be used in default of other things; and that is oak shingles, which get in very few years to look much the same colour as the stone slates, and the roof and the walls go grey together.

The good materials are then, first lead, if you must or may use it, then stone slates, then tiles, then thatch, and lastly, when you can use it, shingles. The bad materials, which nobody ought to use on pain of not being considered an architect at all, are thin slates and Broseley tiles. I can hardly consider that on architect's building the use of these materials is a mere blemish; I look upon it rather as a destruction of the whole building as a work of art.

It seems to me that I have given you pretty well all I had to say on the subject of those rough and homely materials that go to make up our houses. I repeat again, I think it is the most important side of architecture altogether, the choice of material and the use of material. There is another thing to be said about it, that it must lead those people who are really seriously interested in it to interest themselves in the methods of using those materials. That has to do especially with matters like masonry. How does it happen, for example, that a restored building (excuse my mentioning that word) which is very carefully done as to the mouldings and all the rest of it, and is really an absolutely faultless imitation of an Edwardian building, does not look in the faintest degree like an Edwardian building? Many people would say: Because it has got to get old and grey; now it is all new. But I beg to say that is all nonsense; the Edwardian building when brand new did not look like this imitation of the present day. There is no doubt about that, and the reason why it did not look like it is that the whole surface, every moulding, every inch of rubble wall, and what not, was done in a totally different manner; that is to say, the old workmen who did it used to a great extent different tools, and certainly used the tools in a different way. Now if by any possibility the architects could get back the masons and workmen, and what I distinctly call the old scientific method of building walls and surfaces, the really reasonable and scientific method, architecture would to a great extent be on its legs again, and we need not trouble ourselves much about the battle of the styles, if buildings were built in that living manner from beginning to end; out of that the style would arise. We all know of course that you cannot begin by inventing anew, but by attending distinctly to the necessities of the time, and starting at some period, and you must start—you cannot help yourselves—at some period long ago when the art really had roots in it and was not all in the air. Starting with that and attending to the absolute needs of the people who want houses built, and connected with that, with the real solid and genuine use of the material, you would at least get a style which, whatever one may say of it, although it may not build such beautiful buildings as the old buildings, because the whole history of the world has so much changed, would nevertheless produce buildings which would not be ridiculous to the ages which come after us. I am afraid many of those we are building now will be looked upon as mere ingenious toys reflecting a great deal of credit perhaps on the intellect of those who designed them, but very little credit on their good sense and their solidity. You will say that the man was very clever, but he had terrible difficulties to overcome, and he did in a way overcome them after all. But what he has produced, at the very best, is not a building which really forms part of the living shell and skin of the earth on which we live, but is a mere excrescence upon it, a toy which might almost as well, except for the absolute necessity that the people should have a roof to cover them, have remained simply a nicely executed drawing in the architect's office. What we have to get rid of is especially and particularly that. I suppose that the draughtsmanship of the architects of the thirteenth century for their grander buildings was not particularly splendid or complete; I am perfectly certain that a vast number of very beautiful buildings that are built all over the country never had an architect at all, but the roughest possible draught was made out for those buildings, and that they actually grew up simply without any intermediary between the mind and the hands of the people who actually built them. No doubt the great reason why that was so was because the people who built them were traditionally acquainted with the best means of using the materials which happily for them they were forced to use; the materials that were all round about them in the fields and woods amidst which they passed their lives.

Note

1   Built in 1856–9 to the designs of George Gilbert Scott and featuring some very fine ornamental and decorative work, including Morris's Adoration tapestry, designed by Burne-Jones and finished in 1890.

CORRESPONDENCE

TO THE EDITOR OF *The Athenaeum*

March 5, 1877

My eye just now caught the word "restoration" in the morning paper, and, on looking closer, I saw that this time it is nothing less than the Minster of Tewkesbury[1] that is to be destroyed by Sir Gilbert Scott. Is it altogether too late to do something to save it—it and whatever else of beautiful or historical is still left us on the sites of the ancient buildings we were once so famous for? Would it not be of some use once for all, and with the least delay possible, to set on foot an association for the purpose of watching over and protecting these relics, which, scanty as the are now become, are still wonderful treasures, all the more priceless in this age of the world, when the newly-invented study of living history is the chief joy of so many of our lives?

Your paper has so steadily and courageously opposed itself to those acts of barbarism which the modern architect, parson, and squire call "restoration," that it would be waste of words to enlarge here on the ruin that has been wrought by their hands; but, for the saving of what is left, I think I may write a word of encouragement, and say that you by no means stand alone in the matter, and that there are many thoughtful people who would be glad to sacrifice time, money, and comfort in defence of those ancient monuments: besides, though I admit that the architects are, with very few exceptions, hopeless, because interest, habit, and ignorance bind them, and that the clergy are hopeless, because their order, habit, and an ignorance yet grosser, bind them; still there must be many people whose ignorance is accidental rather than inveterate, whose good sense could surely be touched if it were clearly put to them that they were destroying what they, or, more surely still, their sons and sons' sons, would one day fervently long for, and which no wealth or energy could every buy again for them.

What I wish for, therefore, is that an association should be set on foot to keep a watch on old monuments, to protest against all "restoration" that means more than keeping out wind and weather, and, by all means, literary and other, to awaken a feeling that our ancient buildings are not mere ecclesiastical toys, but sacred monuments of the nation's growth and hope.

William Morris

Note

1   The Abbey Church of St Mary at Tewkesbury, Gloucs., was consecrated in 1121. There are additions dating from the mid-thirteenth century onwards, including a splendid lierne vault of the mid-fourteenth century. Morris seems to have been unaware that works on the Abbey had actually started a few years before under the direction of a local builder-*cum*-architect, Thomas Collins, who specialised in the fanciful restoration of half-timbered buildings. At the Abbey he was working partly under the direction of Scott. The 'notice' Morris mentions in this letter was one advertising a fund-raising meeting to be held at Lambeth Palace on 3 March. See A. Jones, *Tewkesbury* (Chichester, 1987), pp. 164-70.

TO THE EDITOR OF *The Times*

April 15, 1878

Sir,

The question asked by Lord Houghton in the House of Lords on Thursday elicited from the Bishop of London an acknowledgement that the scheme proposed some few years back for the wholesale removal of the City churches is continuing its destructive course un-impeded. Four more churches are to be sacrificed to the Mammon-worship and want of taste of this great city. Last year witnessed the destruction of the fine church of St. Michael's, Queenhithe, and All Hallows, Bread-street, which bore upon its walls the inscription stating that Milton had been baptized there. St. Dion's Backchurch, a remarkable building by Wren, is now in course of destruction, while within the last ten years the beautiful church of St. Antholia, with its charming spire, and the skilfully designed little church of St. Mildred, in the Poultry, All Hallows, Staining (except its tower), St. James's, Duke-place, St. Bennet, Gracechurch, with its picturesque steeple, the tower and vestibule of All Hallows-the-Great, Thames-street, have all disappeared. Those for the removal of which a Commission has been now issued are as follows:—St. Margaret Pattens, Roodlane; St. George, Botolph-lane; St. Matthew, Friday-street; and St. Mildred, Bread-street, all works of Wren, and two of them—St. Mildred, Brad-street, and St. Margaret Pattens—possessing spires of singularly original and beautiful design. It must not be supposed that these are the only churches which are in danger, but their proposed destruction serves to show the fate which sooner or later is in store for the whole of Wren's churches in this city, unless Englishmen can be awakened, and by strong and earnest protest show the ecclesiastical authorities that they will not tamely submit to this outrageous and monstrous barbarity.

From an art point of view the loss of these buildings will be irreparable, for Wren's churches form a distinct link in this history of the ecclesiastical art of this country.

Many persons suppose that by preserving St. Paul's Cathedral, that architect's great masterpiece, enough will be left to illustrate his views upon ecclesiastical architecture, but this is far from being the case. For, grand as St. Paul's undoubtedly is, it is only one of a class of buildings common enough on the Continent— imitations of St. Peter's, Rome. In fact, St. Paul's can scarcely be looked upon as an English design, but rather, as an English rendering of the great Italian original, whereas the City churches are examples of purely English renaissance architecture as applied to ecclesiastical purposes, and illustrate a style of architecture peculiar not only to this country but even to this city, and when they are destroyed the peculiar phase of architecture which they exhibit will have ceased to exist, and nothing will be left to record it. The Continent possesses nothing in the least resembling our City churches, and the fact that they are all found in such close proximity to one another only serves to make them the more valuable for purposes of study. One great merit which they possess is shown by the fact that, although they are diminutive in point of size, scarcely any one of them being above 80 ft. long, they possess a dignity of proportion, a masterly treatment as to scale, which renders them far more imposing than many buildings double and treble their dimensions; the relation which they bear to each other and to the great Cathedral which they surround, enhancing by their thin taper spires the importance of the majestic dome, and relieving the dulness and monotony of the general sky line of the City, all serve as unanswerable arguments for their preservation. Surely an opulent city, the capital of the commercial world, can afford some small sacrifice to spare these beautiful buildings the little plots of ground upon which they stand. Is it absolutely necessary that every scrap of space in the City should be devoted to money-making, and are religion, sacred memories, recollections of the great dead, memorials of the past, works of England's greatest architect, to be banished from this wealthy City? If so, alas for our pretended love of art; alas for the English feeling of reverence of which we hear so much; alas for those who are to come after us, whom we shall have robbed of works of art which it was our duty to hand down to them uninjured and unimpaired; alas for ourselves, who will be looked upon by foreign nations and by our own posterity as the only people who have ever lived, who, possessing no architecture of their own, have made themselves remarkable for the destruction of the buildings of their forefathers.

I am, Sir

Your obedient servant,

William Morris,

Hon. Sec., the Society for the

Protection of Ancient Buildings.

TO THE EDITOR OF THE
Daily News

October 31, 1879

I have just received information, on the accuracy of which I can rely, that the restoration of the west front of St. Mark's at Venice, which has long been vaguely threatened, is to be taken in hand at once. A commission is called for next month, to examine its state and to determine whether it is to be pulled down immediately or to be allowed to stand till next year. The fate of such a building seems to me a subject important enough to warrant me in asking you to grant me space to make an appeal to your readers to consider what a disaster is threatened hereby to art and culture in general. Though this marvel of art and treasure of history has suffered some disgraces, chiefly in the base mosaics that have supplanted the earlier ones, it is in the main in a genuine and untouched state, and to the eye of anyone not an expert in building looks safe enough from anything but malice or ignorance. But anyhow, if it be in any way unstable, it is impossible to believe that a very moderate exercise of engineering skill would not make it as sound as any building of its age can be. Whatever pretexts may be put forward, therefore, the proposal to rebuild it can only come from those that suppose that they can renew and better (by imitation) the workmanship of its details, hitherto supposed to be unrivalled; by those that think that there is nothing distinctive between the thoughts, and expression of the thoughts, of the men of the twelfth and of the nineteenth century; by those that prefer gilding, glitter, and blankness, to the solemnity of tone, and the incident that hundreds of years of wind and weather have given to the marble, always beautiful, but from the first meant to grow more beautiful by the lapse of time; in short, those only can think the "restoration" of St. Mark's possible who neither know nor care that it has now become a work of art, a monument of history, and a piece of nature. Surely I need not enlarge on the pre-eminence of St. Mark's in all these characters, for no one who even pretends to care about art, history, or nature, would call it in question; but I will assert that, strongly as I may have seemed to express myself, my words but feebly represent the feelings of a large body of cultivated men who will feel real grief at the loss that seems imminent—a loss which may be slurred over, but which will not be forgotten, and which will be felt ever deeper as cultivation spreads. That the outward aspect of the world should grow uglier day by day in spite of the aspirations of civilisation, nay, partly because of its triumphs, is a grievous puzzle to some of us who are not lacking in sympathy for those aspirations and triumphs, artists and craftsmen as we are. So grievous it is that sometimes we are tempted to say, "Let them make a clean sweep of it all then: let us forget it all, and muddle on as best we may, unencumbered with either history or hope!" But such despair is, we well know, a treason to the cause of civilisation and the arts, and we do our best to overcome it, and to strengthen ourselves in the belief that even a small minority will at last be listened to, and its reasonable opinions be accepted. In this belief I have troubled you with this letter, and I call on all those who share it to join earnestly in any attempt that may be made to save us from an irreparable loss—a loss which only headlong rashness could make possible. Surely it can never be too late to pull down St. Mark's at Venice, the wonder of the civilised world?

SELECT BIBLIOGRAPHY AND FURTHER READING

i) Editions of Morris's own works

Boos, F. (ed.), *William Morris's Socialist Diary* (London: The Journeyman Press, 1985).

Henderson, P. (ed.), *The Letters of William Morris to his Family and Friends* (London: Longmans, 1950).

Kelvin, N. (ed.), *The Collected Letters of William Morris* (4 vols, Princeton, NJ: Princeton University Press, 1984-96).

LeMire, E. (ed.), *The Unpublished Lectures of William Morris* (Detroit: Wayne State University Press, 1969).

Morris, M. (ed.), *The Collected Works of William Morris* (24 vols, London: Longman, Green & Co., 1910-15).

—(ed.), *William Morris: Artist, Writer, Socialist* (2 vols, Oxford: Basil Blackwell, 1936).

Peterson, W.S. (ed.), *The Ideal Book: Essays and Lectures on the Arts of the Book by William Morris* (Berkeley: University of California Press, 1982).

Salmon, N. (ed.), *Political Writings* (Bristol: Thoemmes Press, 1994).

—(ed.), *Journalism* (Bristol: Thoemmes Press, 1996).

ii) Biographies and surveys

Bradley, I., *William Morris and his World* (London: Thames & Hudson, 1978).

Dore, H., *William Morris* (London: Pyramid, 1990).

Faulkner, P. (ed.), *William Morris: The Critical Heritage* (London: Routledge & Kegan Paul, 1973).

—*Against the Age: An Introduction to William Morris* (London: Allen & Unwin, 1980).

Glasier, J.B., *William Morris and the Early Days of the Socialist Movement* (London: Longmans, Green & Co., 1921).

Henderson, P., *William Morris: His Life, Work and Friends* (London, Thames & Hudson, 1967).

Lindsay, J., *William Morris: His Life & Works* (London: Constable, 1975).

MacCarthy, F., *William Morris: A Life for Our Time* (London: Faber & Faber, 1994).

Mackail, J.W., *The Life and Work of William Morris* (2 vols, London: Longmans, 1899).

Poulson, C., *William Morris* (London: The Apple Press, 1989).

Thompson, E.P., *William Morris: Romantic to Revolutionary* (London: Lawrence & Wishart, 1955).

Thompson, P., *The Work of William Morris* (London: Heinemann, 1967).

Vallance, A., *William Morris: His Art, his Writings and his Public Life* (London: George Bell & Sons, 1897).

iii) Works on Morris's family and friends

Burne-Jones, G., *Memorials of Edward Burne-Jones* (2 vols, London: Macmillan, 1904).

Cowley, J., *The Victorian Encounter with Marx: A Study of Ernest Belfort Bax* (London: British Academic Press, 1992).

Faulkner, P. (ed.), *Jane Morris to Wilfrid Scawen Blunt* (Exeter: University of Exeter, 1986).

Fitzgerald, P., *Edward Burne-Jones: A Biography* (London: Michael Joseph, 1975).

Lethaby, W.R., *Philip Webb and his Work* (London: Oxford University Press, 1935).

Marsh, J., *Jane and May Morris: A Biographical Story 1839–1938* (London: Pandora, 1986).

iv) Other important works

Arnot, R.P., *William Morris: A Vindication* (London: Martin Lawrence, 1934).

—*William Morris: The Man and the Myth* (London: Lawrence & Wishart, 1964).

Banham, J. & Harris, J. (eds.), *William Morris and the Middle Ages* (Manchester: Manchester University Press, 1984).

Clark, F., *William Morris: Wallpapers and Chintzes* (London: Academy Editions, 1974).

Cockerell, S. (ed.), *A Note by William Morris on his aims in founding the Kelmscott Press, together with a short history of the press* (London: Kelmscott Press, 1898).

Fairclough, O. & Leary, E., *Textiles by William Morris and Co. 1861–1940* (London: Thames & Hudson, 1981).

Harvey, C. & Press, J., *William Morris, Design and Enterprise in Victorian Britain* (Manchester: Manchester University Press, 1991).

Hodgson, A., *The Romances of William Morris* (London: Cambridge University Press, 1987).

Meier, P., *William Morris: The Marxist Dreamer* (Sussex: Harvester Press, 1978).

Needham, P., *William Morris and the Art of the Book* (London: Oxford University Press, 1976).

Oberg, C., *A Pagan Prophet: William Morris* (Charlottesville: University Press of Virginia, 1978).

Parry, L., *William Morris Textiles* (London: Weidenfeld & Nicolson, 1983).

Peterson, W.S., *The Kelmscott Press: A History of William Morris's Typographical Adventure* (Oxford: Clarendon Press, 1989).

Pevsner, N., *Pioneers of the Modern Movement* (London: Faber & Faber, 1936).

Robinson, D., *William Morris, Burne-Jones and the Kelmscott Chaucer* (London: Fraser, 1982).

Robinson, R., & Wildman, S., *Morris and Company in Cambridge* (Cambridge: Cambridge University Press, 1980).

Sewter, A.C., *The Stained Glass of William Morris and his Circle* (2 vols, New Haven: Yale University Press, 1974–75).

Sparling, H.H., *The Kelmscott Press and William Morris Master-Craftsman* (London: Macmillan, 1924).

Stansky, P., *Redesigning the World: William Morris, the 1880s and the Arts and Crafts Movement* (Princeton NJ: Princeton University Press, 1985).

Watkinson, R., *William Morris as Designer* (London: Studio Vista, 1967).

THE WILLIAM MORRIS SOCIETY

The life, work and ideas of William Morris are as important today as they were in his lifetime. *The William Morris Society* exists to make them as widely known as possible.

The many-sidedness of Morris and the variety of his activities bring together in the *Society* those who are interested in him as designer, craftsman, businessman, poet, socialist, or who admire his robust and generous personality, his creative energy and courage. Morris aimed for a state of affairs in which all might enjoy the potential richness of human life. His thought on how we might live, on creative work, leisure and machinery, on ecology and conservation, on the place of the arts in our lives and their relation to politics, as on much else, remains as challenging now as it was a century ago. He provides a focus for those who deplore the progressive dehumanization of the world in the twentieth-century and who believe, with him, that the trend is not inevitable.

The *Society* provides information on topics of interest to its members and arranges lectures, visits, exhibitions and other events. It encourages the reprinting of his works and the continued manufacture of his textile and wallpaper designs. It publishes a journal twice a year, free to members, which carries articles across the field of Morris scholarship. It also publishes a quarterly newsletter giving details of its programme, new publications and other matters of interest concerning Morris and his circle. Members are invited to contribute items both to the journal and to the newsletter. *The William Morris Society* has a world-wide membership and offers the chance to make contact with fellow Morrisians both in Britain and abroad.

Regular events include a Kelmscott Lecture, a birthday party held in March, and visits to exhibitions and such places as the William Morris Gallery, Red House, Kelmscott Manor and Standen. These visits, our tours and our short residential study courses, enable members living abroad or outside London to participate in the *Society's* activities. The *Society* also has local groups in various parts of Britain and affiliated Societies in the USA and Canada.

For further details, write to:

The Hon. Membership Secretary, Kelmscott House, 26 Upper Mall, Hammersmith, London W6 9TA.